Love Calling

B.J.B Phoenix

www.bjbphoenix.com

Table of Contents

PAPER TOWNS
PUBLISHERS

First Published by
Paper Towns Publishers
72, Vishwanath Dham Colony,
Niwaru Road, Jhotwara,
Jaipur, 302012

AI for Product Managers

ISBN Print Book - 978-93-6185-376-0

Printed in India

Dedication

This book is dedicated to humanity, which seems to be drifting further and further away from its true nature. It is written with the hope of offering a return ticket to those who might have strayed too far and are looking for a way to come back Home.

Gratitude

Thanks to my life partner, who continues to explore the secrets of the universe together with me, sometimes leading, sometimes following. Also to all our children, who continue to teach us about Life and Love in their own unique ways.

And a very special thanks to our first grandson, Kayshav, who reignites Love in all of us with the sparkle in his eyes, every day.

Beneficiary

All author proceeds from this book will be used to directly fund the education of young girls who find themselves in under-privileged circumstances. More information can be found on EducateEveryGirl.com.

The Universal Dance

Love awakens with a smile
Life sprouts into furious action
Light, Passion, Darkness chase each other
Losing, winning, making, breaking
Listening, speaking, strolling, sprinting
Laughing, crying, sleeping, waking
Leading, trailing, friending, fighting
Losing sight of Life that vibrates within
Letting ignorance drive the ego
Longing for Love to heal

Prologue

As a child, Kiara had learnt to keep her emotions to herself. No one understood. Not even her friends. They were all happy to just wait for the time when they will find a husband and spend the rest of their lives taking care of their families. She sighed in despair. She didn't even know how to put into words what she felt most of the time. It was like a spirit trapped in a body, desperately trying to fly free.

From the time that she could remember, Kiara's most favorite moments in life had been her birthdays. Every birthday, her father would give her and her twin brother Kaanja one of his newly invented toys. She was always given something 'appropriate' for girls. Growing up, she would often ask her mother about who had decided what was appropriate for whom? Since she never received a satisfactory response, at some point she had stopped asking.

Kaanja never showed any interest in the toys he got; he would always just give them to her. That expectation always doubled her excitement as she waited for each birthday. For several weeks after their birthday, Kiara would take apart the toys carefully and reassemble them back, always starting with the one that was 'appropriate' for her brother. After her tampering, sometimes the toys would still work as intended, sometimes they wouldn't. Whenever she reassembled one successfully the first time around, she felt extremely proud of herself.

She never had the courage to tell her father that she would like to work with him in his toy business, that she would like to see and learn what he did and how hc did it. Her ambition had nothing to do with getting married and having a family. Her ambition was to invent new toys. She had so many great ideas that she wanted to put to the test.

Even though it was the twenty first century and women had moved gigantic steps forward in many parts of the world, almost every girl around Kiara seemed quite content to follow the local social norm that had been in place for centuries.

Not Kiara though; she was constantly fighting with someone or the other in her own mind for her lack of freedom.

Note:
The prologue is an excerpt from the author's previous book: Life Calling

1

No Time for Love

Kiara found her loudest voice and yelled, "Just get out!" She then slammed the door on his face, shocking herself into dead silence for several minutes.

She just stood there with her eyes getting bigger as the minutes ticked by. Finally, a proud smile started to spread across her beautiful face. She walked across her small apartment and threw herself into her favorite spot, a gigantic bean bag chair.

Wow! she mused with her smile getting wider, I didn't know I had that in me!

Before she could process her behavior further, her phone rang. She looked at the caller ID and her smile became childishly mischievous as she answered the call.

"What have you done now?" asked Kaanja in his typical lazy tone.

Kiara laughed, "What do you mean?" Kaanja was her twin brother, and this was the special connection they shared. Kaanja always seemed to just know when significant emotional shifts were taking place in his sister's life. They were both in their second year of college in different cities, but distance was no obstacle for their closeness.

"Come on, out with it!" It was clear from Kaanja's tone that he was not going to be dissuaded from finding out.

Kiara saw no point in denying anything; it would only delay the inevitable because Kaanja was not going to give up until he got the truth. He was only five minutes older than her, but often behaved like he was her father and needed to protect her from the world. He had a lot to do with Kiara being allowed to leave home and go away to college, so he probably felt responsible for making sure she wasn't getting into any trouble.

"You remember how you always worried in high school that some guy would take advantage of me, and I told you not to worry 'cuz when I fall for someone it would be a mature, tall, dark, and handsome gentleman and not some immature high school kid? Well, I met him."

"Ooh so you've found your true love," Kaanja tried to sound excited.

"True love, my foot!" retorted Kiara. "It took me all of two months to realize what a jerk he is."

"Oh, I'm sorry?" Kaanja wasn't sure how to respond since his sister didn't seem upset in any way. Deep down though, he felt relieved since he preferred for his sister not to get distracted from her career goals. He had always believed that there was a right time for engaging in different types of experiences in one's life, and it was for us to choose these times wisely. In his view, this was not the right time for his sister to engage in anything but finishing her education and shaping her career goals.

"No you're not," said Kiara confidently. "You're relieved that there's no one to distract me from my studies and get me into trouble."

"Listen, Dude, I've full faith in you, but this is the first time you've received so much freedom in your life. You wanna stretch your wings, I get it, but please keep your priorities straight. There's no need to rush into anything. Just keep your head firmly on your shoulders, your feet firmly on the ground, and your eyes on your immediate goal."

Kiara smiled affectionately as she hung up the phone. It felt like she and Kaanja had been siblings since the beginning of time; the underlying love never seemed to fade.

❖

Kiara sank into her bean-bag chair again with a whole box of chocolate fudge ice cream in her hands and recalled the day she had been totally swept off her feet without warning.

It was the annual meet-and-greet party of the engineering club. Kiara had spent most of her first year in college dedicating herself fully to her studies and topping every class with the highest grades. In her second year, she had allowed her friend Zen to convince her to join the engineering club, more to add some social interactions in her life than anything else.

She relived the sense of discomfort she had felt on that first day of the club meeting, in a room full of mainly male students. Many interested glances had immediately come her way. In a crowd of more than a hundred, she counted no more than five females. It had taken her less than five minutes to decide that this was not for her; she had more important things to do with her life.

She recalled hearing the president of the club announcing the main guest for the evening as she was making her way towards the exit. The CEO of some highly successful start-up company. Thinking that it might seem rude for her to walk out just at that moment, she had turned around and found herself staring directly into a pair of deep green eyes on the stage. She had felt her heart skip a beat, or two, as she noticed in that split-second the dark strands of hair falling on the wide forehead of an exotically honey-colored face with a crooked one-sided smile. She had felt a shocking shiver run down her spine.

Thankfully, before she could have done anything to make a total fool of herself, the deep green eyes had turned away as the owner of those eyes had proceeded to take the microphone, calmly unscrewing the stand to raise it to his height before starting to speak.

There was no sneaking away at that point since the room had become totally quiet. In any case, she would have been unable to move as her legs had suddenly gotten glued to the ground.

The guest had started his speech by acknowledging and congratulating the very few female students in the room, his eyes once again locking with Kiara's. She had no recollection of what else was said. She only remembered how impressed she had been with his words on the need for increasing the number of women in engineering.

What a hypocrite! she said out loud as she stuffed another big spoon-ful of ice cream into her mouth, then continued her recollection. At some point during that evening she had found herself talking to him, thankfully relieved that the topics had revolved around new developments in the field of engineering. He had said it would be great to meet up for coffee one day and discuss more, so she had given him her phone number.

That's how it had started. They had met for coffee a couple of days later but there had been no mention of engineering; instead, a lot of remarks had been made about how it was all good for women to get a degree, but ultimately their focus had to be on managing a family to sustain the social order. Every time he had made a remark like that, Kiara's life-long emotions of resentment had threatened to break loose, but she had always kept her calm with polite silence.

Today was supposed to be the fourth time they were going to go out for dinner. When he came to pick her up, he had authoritatively made himself comfortable on the sofa, looked at her in what to her was quite weird, and said, "Why don't we just stay here and you can cook us up some dinner?" He had then gotten up, walked over to her, given her a highly uncomfortable touch on the cheek and added, "It will be a lot more fun." His eyes had un-ashamedly insinuated a lot more to emphasize the meaning behind his words as he had tried to pull her closer to him.

The rest was now history. Kiara stuffed her mouth with some more ice cream. She felt like this was her second awakening in terms of standing her ground. The first one had been two years ago in high school during her class presentation where she had finally mustered up the courage to face her fear of public speaking.

She lounged in her bean bag just savoring the ice cream for a long time. This was going to be an important day in her life journey. Once the ice cream was done, she started reflecting on how this experience was actually going to impact on her future decisions.

She had heard and read a lot about love-at-first-sight, and in the beginning her heart had been naive and romantic enough to believe that that was what had happened to her; but now she thought with her brain. How can you be in love with someone that you don't even know? No matter how strong the physical response to anyone, how can it be love without any data to support the feeling? If you start a relationship believing you are in love with someone you don't even know, then you will have already created an image of that person which, in your mind, passes the test of every single subjective criteria you hold of perfection. If that's where the relationship starts, then the only way for it to go is down-the-tube as you discover each aspect that does not pass the test in reality.

The analysis led her to the conclusion that love is something that must start from zero and then build over time as you discover the compatible elements in the relationship. As soon as the compatible aspects overtake the incompatible ones, the relationship can be called a success, because in her view, perfect compatibility had to be a myth, especially in married life.

Yes, that was it. She felt satisfied with her conclusion. She would make sure to stay away from anything in her life that started with a strong physical reaction, good or bad, or at least handle such situations more intelligently by first collecting the facts and analyzing her emotions before making any decisions.

In any case, she told herself, she had a lot more important things to deal with in her life and it was going to take a lot of her attention to achieve her goals. She had no time for love right now.

Flavors of Love

SIBLING

When nights were dark, the path unknown
You held my hand and led the way
Then gave me wings to call my own
And whispered softly Fly Away!

2

To Love or Not to Love

Raindrops stormed down in unison over the ocean, as if to prove their superiority in maintaining the Earth's ecosystem. The ocean seemed to simply smile in response by creating a small circular ripple every time a drop hit it. Perhaps the drops had forgotten that they owed their existence to this ocean. Or perhaps they hadn't. Perhaps what appeared as arrogance to the observing eye was actually the impatience of the raindrops to reunite with their source.

Kiara and Zen sat on a rock with their legs dangling, feet in water, silently enjoying getting drenched in the summer rain. The mesmerizing interactions between the rain and the ocean continued in front of their eyes, sometimes looking like a battle with angry waves crashing against the shores, and sometimes like a playful dance between the drops and the ripples.

The rain stopped as abruptly as it had started. Kiara looked at Zen and wondered if parents somehow end up steering the personality development of a child through the naming process. The fact that you are bombarded by that given name throughout your life perhaps results in manifesting the corresponding behavior. Zen was the first close friend Kiara had made in college and she had yet to see her friend ever getting flustered in any situation, big or small.

"Are you sure about this?" Kiara finally broke the silence. "I mean, you don't even know him but you're ready to spend the rest of your life with him?"

Zen gave Kiara an impish smile. "Of course I'm ok with this. This is how I always imagined it. I always knew there was someone that the Universe had planned for me, and I was sure he'd show up in my life when the time was right. Why should it matter whether my parents found him or I did?"

Kiara thought for a minute, then said, "But what about love? Don't you think it's important to make sure that you can love the person before you get married?"

"What's not to love?" countered Zen. "I met him a couple times. He's good looking and a real gentleman. I like him. He'll be my husband. Of course I will grow to love him."

Kiara was not convinced. “Love is not something you can choose to feel at will,” she insisted. “It’s either there or it isn’t.”

“No, Kiara,” Zen looked at her friend a bit more seriously. “Love is always there. Always. We choose to restrict its definition to specific physical reactions which are driven by our personal, social and mental programming. We respond favorably to someone who meets our expectations and call it love. Once we find out things about the person that do not meet our expectations, we decide we no longer love them.”

“Are you sure you’re as old as you say you are?” Kiara looked at Zen with fake suspicion, “Sometimes you talk like an ancient sage.”

“I prefer to be known as the ‘modern sage in a mini-skirt’,” Zen responded in a deep voice while shifting into a lotus position, her right hand going up in a blessing gesture. “Listen carefully, child,” she continued her imitation, “Real love is not something that is dependent on another person’s behavior. The key is acceptance. Once you accept someone in your life as family, you love them like you love other people in your life, like parents or siblings, irrespective of how they behave. ”

"But that's different!" Kiara smiled at Zen's performance, but was not ready to give up. "You have a blood connection with people you're related to. Of course you'll love them."

"Do we really always love them though?" Zen was not ready to give up either. "How long does it take for us not to love them once we find out they're abusive, or exploiting us, or just don't care about us because they're selfish?" She put her feet back in the water and adopted her normal tone. "In any case, if you start at the beginning of evolution, we're all connected by blood, but it hasn't stopped us from fighting wars because we believe in different things, or have different sounding names, or speak different languages. Since the beginning of humanity we have been choosing who we are going to love and who not, and why or why not. As long as a person serves our interest or makes us feel good, we love them. As soon as we start to see the flaws we no longer feel the same way. We're all selfish that way, so what we claim to feel is not real love."

"Wow!" Kiara was visibly shocked, "I had no idea you had so much cynicism in you!"

"It's not cynicism," Zen responded with genuine sincerity. "Just stating facts. When you grow up in a big joint family living in a small space, you get a crash-course in human psychology. I learnt early in life that it's better to accept the facts as you observe them and then manage your expectations accordingly, rather than delude yourself with how you wish things to be. It makes life much simpler. Just choose to love and overlook the small stuff at the physical level as normal human behavior."

"But why would you choose to love someone who makes your life miserable?" Kiara asked, amazed at how so much depth could have been hiding behind thc lighthearted Zen she had known thus far.

"Loving someone doesn't mean you allow them to get away with anything that you feel isn't right. In fact, you must always take a stand against what you genuinely consider to be wrong; stand-up for your own well-being if it's being unfairly compromised by someone else. This has nothing to do with loving or not loving someone. It's a whole different issue. You must take a stand against injustice, no question. What Love does is give you the strength to do the 'right' thing without generating unnecessary negativity for yourself. You might even unknowingly end up helping the person to evolve in a positive manner."

Both fell silent again. The raindrops started their dance with the ocean once again, as if they had stopped only to listen to the conversation between the two friends.

Although Kiara's heart was filled with a new-found respect for Zen, she still wasn't convinced that Zen was doing the right thing by agreeing to an arranged marriage. Kiara tried to find examples that would disprove Zen's theory about love, while Zen sat there with a slight smile on her face mesmerized by the ripples all over again, totally immersed in the moment.

Kiara thought about her own experience. Her own theory of love had fallen flat on its face. What she had felt, no matter how intense, had certainly proved not to be love, because had it been, it would not have evaporated within two months. Although she had not 'chosen' to feel the way she had felt initially, she could understand how she was actually choosing not to feel the same way about him now because of all that she knew about him. The person was still the same as he had been when she first saw him; it was her feelings that had changed based on information coming into her brain.

She looked at her friend and wondered how it felt to just accept another person without any judgement, and then be prepared to love them for who they are.

"What if he doesn't respect you for who you are?" she asked when the rain suddenly stopped again. "I think that's more important than even love. I can agree that perhaps you can grow to love someone who respects you as an individual, but what if he doesn't? What if he's one of those who believes in different roles for women and men? What if he gets violent when he drinks? What if he doesn't allow you to have a career?"

Zen considered Kiara's questions quietly for a long time. Such was the relationship between these two friends - they could be in each other's company comfortably for hours without saying a word.

Zen finally broke the silence. "What guarantee is there that the same situations will not arise if I marry someone I think I know well? Things are always different after marriage no matter who you marry. I've seen all kinds of marriages in my family; realities of life overtake everything else. You just need to deal with life as it unfolds. I know my parents have done their due diligence in selecting a person for me. I like what I've seen of him so far; I think we can figure out the rest as it happens." She then looked at Kiara with her impish smile again. "But if he does get violent after drinking, I can always call you for help. We'll beat the drink out of him together!"

With that, Zen scooped up some water in her hands and threw it playfully at Kiara. She then got up and ran back to the car knowing that Kiara was going to reciprocate if she stayed.

Kiara allowed her to run away safely. It was the final week of their college and soon they will go their separate ways. No matter where they ended up in their lives, Kiara knew that Zen will always remain one of her closest friends because she felt the same unfading love for her as she did for Kaanja, even in the short time that she had know her. As she watched Zen get into the car, a startling thought ran through her body: could it actually be the exact same Love that just manifests differently in different bodies for different experiences? Is it possible that real Love is something that is accessible to us all from beyond us?

As she got up to go, she pondered on what Zen had said earlier: *Love is always there. Always.*

Then why would anyone ever choose not to love, Kiara wondered silently as she walked slowly to the car.

Flavors of Love

NATURE

Illustrated by Cynthia Medranda

The tree and I
We stand as One
I breathe in
What it breathes out.
The birds,
They seem to sing through me
To make the seeds of blossom sprout.

3

Ego: The Enemy of Love

As the plane came to a stop in front of the gate, Kiara unlocked her seatbelt and took out her backpack from the cabin above. Although dressed casually in her faded jeans and white crop top, her five feet/eight inches height and the thick bouncy brown hair framing her beautiful features resulted in many second glances from fellow passengers. She had an overall elegant persona that was hard to ignore and drew admiring looks from anyone who laid eyes on her.

Totally unaware of her own appeal, she got off the plane with a slight frown on her normally smiling face. It was almost five years since she had last seen Lucy. It was also five years since Kiara had taken over her Dad's toy business after completing her accelerated MBA. Her Dad had shown incredible trust and confidence in Kiara's capabilities by handing her the ropes right after she finished her education, and Kiara had been giving the business everything she had in order to make sure she didn't let her

Dad down. She had been so busy that her social life had been reduced to simply keeping in touch with her closest friends through occasional video calls.

Lucy was one of those friends who went back to Kiara's high school days. She was among those where it didn't matter how long it had been since they last spoke; they knew they could count on each other no matter when and where. They had ended up in different colleges because of their career interests, but luckily their desire to move to the same city had worked out, which had allowed them to regularly do outings during their undergraduate days until Kiara had to move again for her MBA.

While walking out to get a taxi, a soft smile spread across Kiara's face as she recalled their last meeting at Lucy's wedding five years ago. It was the most beautiful event Kiara had ever attended. Lucy and Nikos had met in college and Nikos had proposed to her on their graduation day before they had to return back to their homes. Nikos had conspired with Kiara to plan the proposal, making sure that a rejection was not in the cards. The wedding had taken place one year later since Lucy had made it clear that she was not getting married without her maid of honor who needed to complete her MBA first, and she herself needed that time to plan a perfect wedding in any case.

And a perfect wedding it had been.

Which is exactly why Kiara had been utterly shocked when she got a call from Lucy yesterday saying she wanted a divorce. She had added that she wanted Kiara to be there when she broke the news to Nikos. Kiara had immediately cancelled all her meetings to get on the first flight out from Japan, where she had been attending a conference, to Greece, where Lucy had settled down in her married life.

As the taxi made its way down the motorway, Kiara tried to recall her conversations with Lucy over the past five years. There was certainly no way based on those conversations that Kiara could have seen this coming. As far as she could recall, Lucy had never mentioned anything about any marital problem. She had always been her cheerful self, talking about her adventures with Nikos, their trips to other countries, even family planning. Granted that it was almost three months since they had last talked, but still, such decisions are not made suddenly over a couple of months, are they?

❖

The two friends sat sipping coffee on the dining table in the spacious three-bedroom apartment. The excitement of seeing each other and being able to hug each other again was so overpowering that Kiara had actually forgotten for a while why she was here.

She now looked at Lucy with her piercing eyes trying to read what might be the reason behind Lucy's unhappiness.

A thick silence started to descend between them with the unasked question hanging in the middle. Kiara allowed the silence to prevail as Lucy just stared into her coffee. Kiara didn't want to rush her in any way; she knew Lucy will open up whenever she felt ready.

"I miss home!" Lucy blurted after awhile. "I left everything behind thinking nothing matters as long as Nikos and I are together."

Another silence fell between them. As Kiara waited for Lucy to continue, her mind drifted back to what Zen had said to her many years ago: *things are always different after marriage no matter who you marry. Realities of life overtake everything else. You just need to deal with life as it unfolds.*

She only felt admiration for how Zen had managed to retain such a mature understanding of life from her own observations. Kiara felt totally incapable of advising Lucy on what to do; she was here only to listen and provide moral support. Somewhere at the back of her mind, though, she knew what she could do to help Lucy untangle her situation if it became necessary.

Another five minutes passed with nothing but the sound of sipping coffee. Finally, Lucy looked up at Kiara and said with a smile, "You know, it feels good to just say it out loud to someone. It's been eating away at me just thinking about it constantly."

"Being homesick is a very normal feeling, Lucy," Kiara commented when it didn't seem like anything more was going to come from the other side. "We were so homesick when we left home to go to college in another city, remember? You left your whole country behind when you came here. Of course you feel homesick."

Lucy simply smiled but said nothing, so Kiara continued, "Have you mentioned this to Nikos?"

"No," was Lucy's response. Then, "You would think that he would notice how I'm feeling, but he hasn't asked me once what's the matter!"

If there was one thing Kiara had tested and confirmed for herself over the past five years of her life, it was the importance of open communication. No relationship, be it family, business, or friends can survive a serious lack of communication. This was something Kaanja had ingrained into her since she was very young. Her brother was the only person Kiara knew whose wisdom exponentially surpassed his limited years on earth.

Just because you're thinking something in my presence doesn't mean I know what you're thinking, Kaanja would say *repeatedly. Most of us are not blessed with the talent of mind-reading. If you're thinking it and you want me to know it, repeat: if you want me to know it, then say it. Just follow these three rules in life and it'll simplify everything for you: communicate, communicate again, and communicate some more! There is absolutely no problem on this earth that an adult, mature dialogue cannot solve. But remember to always communicate with love and understanding. Don't assume and don't judge. Just communicate what you want someone to know.*

Kiara would always counter him with: *It's not as simple as you make it sound. What if the other person is adult but not mature? What if the other person doesn't like what you're saying and starts a fight?*

Who're we to judge maturity? Kaanja would ask. *Everyone is the way they need to be for their own growth. Our job is to do our part based on* **our** *maturity. Once we're clear in our conscience that we've done our part as maturely as we're able, we can then take decisions based on the response we get. There's nothing wrong with agreeing to disagree and follow separate paths in life if that's what seems best for both parties. Compromise is needed only when both parties mutually want to coexist within a certain common boundary.*

You mean like families? Kiara would ask.

Yes, like families, or close friends. If I don't see eye-to-eye with Dad about my career, for example, then I just need to decide whether I want to follow a separate path to make my life, or compromise because it's more important for me to coexist with him. This is where love comes into the picture. You relinquish your ego and make compromises for the sake of love, instead of trying to prove who's right and who's wrong. Not ***sacrifices****, which are done under pressure and only make you miserable, but* ***compromises*** *that are made willingly for the sake of love because you enjoy sharing your life with these people. The point though is that unless I communicate my perspective to him, I won't really know whether we can find common ground, or whether he'd be willing to make some compromises for me as well. No matter what our differences, I don't doubt at all his love for me. By discussing, we might come to a solution that works for everyone and no compromises may even be necessary.*

Kiara looked at Lucy and wondered where love was in all this right now. It had been there one hundred percent five years ago. Where was it now? As if Zen had somehow heard her from far away, her words rang in Kiara's ears again: *Love is always there. Always.*

Before Kiara could ask anything more, Lucy continued, "Nikos has his family here. He gets to go and spend time with them every so often. He'll never understand what I'm feeling. I know he'll never leave his family for me. Why should I be the one to sacrifice everything?!"

"Do you still love him?" Kiara asked when Lucy fell silent again, recalling Kaanja's words about sacrifices versus compromises.

Lucy thought for a moment before replying honestly, "I don't know anymore. All I'm feeling right now is that I'm the only one who's making all the sacrifices. No family, no career, no real friends. Nikos is always busy with his work, but of course always finds time for his family. I'm the one expected to make all the adjustments. Why?"

A touch of bitterness had crept into Lucy's tone as tears started to well-up in her eyes. Kiara stood up and gave her friend a hug, holding her head tightly against her chest and just allowing her to cry for as long as she needed to. She couldn't help but feel a sense of angst against Nikos for what he seemed to have done to her friend. Kiara had never seen Lucy cry before and it wrenched her heart to see her like this.

When Lucy had run out of tears, she disengaged herself and looked up at Kiara. "I'm sorry, this is not how this was supposed to go. Why don't you go freshen up. You must be tired from your flight. I'll get lunch ready."

As Kiara sat in her room thinking what to do, she decided to go forward with her plan to help Lucy. There was only one person who could guide them through this: Kaanja. All three of them had been good friends during high school, so Kiara knew that Lucy wouldn't mind her sharing this with her brother. In fact, everyone who knew Kaanja agreed that he was the go-to person for any life advice.

When she called Kaanja and told him what was going on, he had only this to say: "How much do you wanna bet that Nikos thinks he's the one making all the adjustments in this marriage? I'm sure multiple layers of ego have built-up on both sides and love is no longer visible. All you have to do is facilitate the peeling process."

Flavors of Love

FRIEND

Illustrated by Cynthia Medranda

The trust we shared
The stunts we dared
Emotions bared
Tempers flared
Yet still we cared.

4

Ego: The Enemy of Love (Yes, again)

Nikos walked into the apartment as Kiara and Lucy were having a really late lunch. He gave Lucy a kiss on the cheek and then turned to Kiara.

"Welcome! Lucy told me you were coming. It's a pleasure to have you, and I'm sure it'll do wonders for Lucy. I think she's been feeling a bit lonely lately."

Lucy seemed almost startled at his remark, a reaction which Nikos failed to see because he was facing Kiara. Kiara tried not to judge him while she gave him a friendly hug. She had met Nikos enough times to have developed a level of comfort in his presence, and she actually liked him. Right now though, she felt an awkwardness given the situation. This was the person making her friend miserable; she didn't want to like him. Then she reminded herself that this is also the person who had brought the most happiness in her friend's life. She couldn't help feeling a bit sorry since he obviously had no idea why she was here.

It was actually very difficult not to like Nikos. He was charming, polite, and had matured into a true gentleman. They talked about college days, about the work that Nikos was doing, about Kiara's business, about all that Kiara must see while she was here. Even Lucy got excited about the prospect of sightseeing and started planning an itinerary for the next day. The overall atmosphere and energy in the room was so friendly and positive that no-one realized where the time flew until Lucy got up and exclaimed in horror, "Oh Dear, I'm such a bad host. I need to go get dinner ready."

"I'll come help, what are we making?" Kiara got up but Lucy held up her hand.

"No, you stay here and finish up the planning for tomorrow. I have everything prepped for lasagna. I just need to put it all together and put it in the oven. I won't be long." With that she left the room and went to the kitchen.

Nikos finished the itinerary with instruction on where he will meet them for dinner at the end of the day. He wanted her to try some amazing authentic Greek food. He then poured three glasses of wine, handed one to Kiara, took one to the kitchen for Lucy, and then came back and sat down across from her with his own glass in hand.

"She's almost done," he updated on the state of affairs in the kitchen, and then more seriously, "I'm really glad you're here. I feel Lucy needs a change. Life has perhaps become a bit too monotonous lately for her. I have my work that keeps me busier than I'd like, but I need to get a lot done to get us settled into a comfortable life." He looked around the apartment and added, "I mean it's not bad what we have, but it takes a lot even to maintain this. Between my work, Lucy, and my parents, it just takes everything out of me trying to balance everything," he smiled wistfully. "There's just no energy left to do anything extra, let alone travel like we used to before. I'm glad Lucy will have some distraction for some time at least. How long are you staying?"

Kiara tried to sound casual. It was clear he had no idea what was going on in Lucy's mind. "I don't know. I've left my return ticket open for now. I think it's time I take a break from work for a bit," she sighed with a smile, "it's been very hectic the last five years."

Thankfully, Lucy walked in at that moment, a genuine spark of happiness in her eyes as she said, "That's so correct. You definitely need a break. I'm not letting you go anytime soon!" It was almost like she had forgotten why she had called Kiara in the first place.

It doesn't really seem so bad, Kiara thought to herself as they ate their dinner and she witnessed the friendly banter between Lucy and Nikos. There was no doubt that they were enjoying each other's company. Kiara felt a bit confused. Maybe Kaanja, as usual, was actually right. Maybe it was just the layers of ego that reared their ugly head in Lucy's mind when she was alone with nothing to keep her busy. Kaanja had certainly predicted one thing accurately: Nikos felt he was bearing the more stressful responsibility of providing a comfortable life for his family. It seemed the time he spent with his parents also felt more like an obligation that he was trying to fulfill. In his mind, he was living his life for other people, doing everything for their benefit. No wonder he felt exhausted.

Lucy turned to Kiara with a happy smile. "This is the first time in months that Nikos and I are actually having dinner together," she said while giving Nikos an accusing glance, "and it's all thanks to you. He came home early only because he knew you were coming."

Nikos got up with all the dirty plates in his hands to put in the sink. "Well, someone's got to make sure there'll always be food on the table you know," was his remark.

Kaanja was definitely right. There was plenty of ego going around between Lucy and Nikos, but all in their own heads. There had apparently been zero communication between them on any of these topics. Each was gratifying their own ego by believing they were contributing more to the marriage and expecting that the other should have nothing to complain about. Each of them had convinced themselves that if anyone in the marriage was unhappy, it was the other person's fault.

Once Nikos had left for work the next morning, Kiara made it clear that there was no way she was going to enjoy any sightseeing with this big elephant in the room. They needed to deal with it first, and that meant having a video call with Kaanja.

Kaanja's ruggedly good-looking face filled the computer screen as he used his fingers to get his overgrown hair in some order. It was still very early morning for him and it was clear that, although awake because he had been expecting Kiara's call, he had not yet fully committed to getting out of bed.

Kaanja sat up against the pillows with his phone in hand; he was not one to aimlessly chitchat. After exchanging the initial pleasantries, he got right down to business.

"Lucy," his calm, husky voice was amazingly soothing to hear, "just close your eyes, take a deep breath and relax."

Lucy followed the instruction without hesitation. "Now imagine you are divorced and back here with your parents, who by the way have moved on in their own lives filling the gap you left behind, but let's imagine it's all exactly the same as you left it. You get up every morning and do whatever you imagine you'll be doing during the day." He paused for a few seconds to let his words sink in, then continued, "How does it feel? Are you happy?"

"No," was Lucy's response after due consideration.

"Why not? Isn't that what you are craving?"

"I'll miss not having Nikos around," Lucy replied with a touch of sadness.

"So you just want to run away from one unhappy situation to another one?" Kaanja asked. "If your answer had been yes, I would have told Kiara to immediately help you pack your bags. But think about it, Lucy. Life is not about looking back and trying to recreate a status quo. It's about moving forward and creating a new life for ourselves every moment. You made the compromises you made because you wanted to share the rest of your life with Nikos. Don't turn them into sacrifices now."

Another silence fell to allow Lucy to assess her thoughts.

Then Kaanja continued, "Love is our true nature, Lucy; it is always there. It's a lucky event when we meet someone where it is able to shine brightly because there are no expectations and judgments, just acceptance of the other person and support for the choices they make in their life to create their own unique experiences. This is when Love is able to experience itself fully through us. You're lucky to have found such a person where Love is able to shine through both of you at the same time. Don't cover it up with layers of egotistical thoughts."

"But I can't help the way I feel!" Lucy's tone was now tinged with a sense of hopelessness.

"Of course you can," was Kaanja's calm response, surprising even Kiara. "Feelings are nothing more than reflections of our thoughts. Think happy thoughts, and you'll feel happy. Think sad thoughts, you'll feel sad. Think angry thoughts, you'll feel angry. If you don't believe me, you can experiment yourself. Think about your wedding day. I can see it all so clearly. What a beautiful event it was!"

A smile spread across Lucy's face as she recalled her wedding day, her eyes still closed. Each of them recalled that day in nostalgic silence for a few minutes. "I love Nikos," she murmured softly.

"I know that," said Kaanja. "I saw it from day one. But if I now fill your head with thoughts of how he doesn't appreciate you, you'll be confused again. Drop the layers, Lucy. Be open and transparent. Talk to him about what you feel is missing in your life, and what can be done about it. There's always a solution when all parties are open to finding a solution. Perhaps he might be feeling under-appreciated as well. The reality is that someone's behavior towards us is directly impacted by how we behave towards them. It's always a good idea to reflect on how we may be contributing to the other person's behavior, and then communicate with an awareness of that insight."

Kaanja gave Lucy a few moments to reflect, then continued, "You both decided to share your lives with each other, so you need to share all that makes up our lives: thoughts, feelings, desires, ambitions. Adult and mature communication is always the key to a comfortable coexistence, and all I mean by mature communication is that it needs to be a two-way street where listening can often be by far the more effective side of the street than talking."

Another silence fell. Lucy opened her eyes and just sat there, deep in thought. After a few minutes, Kaanja continued.

"Our thoughts determine our actions, and those actions shape our lives, Lucy. Your thoughts and actions of the past have shaped your present. Your thoughts and actions now will shape your future. We can think whatever we want, no one can stop us, but we must think very carefully about our actions because actions can have long-lasting repercussions and cannot be undone. So all I can advise right now is that please don't make any rash decisions. Be absolutely sure about what action you want to take."

With that Kaanja signed off, leaving the two girls to think about everything he had said. Kiara went to her room and took a long time to get ready for their outing; she wanted to give Lucy some space to reflect if she wanted to. When she she finally went back out, she saw Lucy putting some snacks in a backpack in the kitchen.

"I can't even imagine my life without Nikos," Lucy said firmly when she saw Kiara. "I've been engrossing myself so completely in my negative thoughts all day long that I completely lost touch with the bigger picture."

Kiara said nothing, but she felt the uplifting energy in the room. Lucy walked over to her and gave her a tight hug. "I'm so lucky to have friends like you and Kaanja," she said, then added, "I know Nikos doesn't have an easy life either. He really works hard to keep it all together. We just need to talk it through and find a solution for both of us, but that's for me to deal with together with my husband. As for you, you've got some sightseeing to do. I can't wait to show you how amazing this country is!"

Flavors of Love

SPOUSE

Perhaps there are more downs than ups
Perhaps sometimes more dark than light
But every turn we take in life, here we are, side by side.

5

Love is Always There

Ever since returning from Greece almost three months ago, Kiara had been unable to shake off a deeply unsettling thought that kept creeping up in her mind at the most uncomfortable moments.

Right now was one of those moments. She sat across from one of her employees who it was discovered had been taking kick-backs for office supply contracts. She tried her best to control the feeling of being betrayed. She suddenly recalled her first experience with the so-called falling in love phenomenon and the emotion that surfaced towards that person was a sense of dislike. As if suddenly thrown into the twilight zone, she then recalled this girl next door who was constantly blasting loud music, and the only emotion that surfaced for her was annoyance, to put it mildly.

Kiara could count on her fingers the people in her life where the default underlying emotion that surfaced was love when she thought about them. For everyone else, it ranged from plain indifference to utterly intolerable.

There is just no way that love is always there and that it's us who choose not to feel it, she thought to herself. *No way. And why should we always feel it for everyone anyways? They don't deserve it always. Love must be earned!*

There it was again, those deeply unsettling words ringing in her ears: *Love is always there. Always.*

She had heard it from two of the wisest people she knew in her entire life. She might have written-off Zen as still naive, but Kaanja? He was anything but naive. To the contrary, his understanding of how Life works seemed like an accumulation of thousands of lifetimes. Kiara had never really bought into the theory of reincarnation, but every time she observed Kaanja in action, it did make her wonder. He was too young in this lifetime to know all that he did.

Kiara never ignored anything that Kaanja had to say, because he never said anything unless he felt strongly that it needed to be said. His intentions behind saying it were never selfish. It didn't really matter to him whether anyone believed him or not. He never tried to prove his point. He would say it and move on with his life, while everyone else would spend hours arguing about what he had said and whether it was true.

She looked at the employee across from her and tried to imagine how Kaanja would handle this situation. The guy just sat there quietly, his eyes on his fidgeting hands. After a while Kiara just gave up trying to adjust her behavior based on those deeply unsettling words of wisdom. Right was right. Rules were rules. The guy had done something wrong, and the consequences must be faced. She handed him his termination letter quietly and walked out of the room. She had a lot to say to him, but deep down she knew that it would change nothing; she would be venting only for her own satisfaction, and then feel exhausted.

She was definitely going to say a lot to Kaanja, though, the next time she saw him. She needed to get on with her life without this annoying weight of his wisdom hanging over her head!

❖

The opportunity to have a face-to-face with Kaanja presented itself sooner than Kiara had expected. Her phone rang as soon as she entered her hotel room in Jaipur, India, where she had just concluded a day of exhausting meetings with a group of potential wholesale clients in the Asia region for the launch of her new toy.

"Your timing is perfect," was how she answered the call, "I just got into my room." She and Kaanja never wasted words on pleasantries; it never felt like there had been any gap between their phone calls, even though it had been at least two weeks this time around given Kiara's busy schedule and them being in different time zones.

"I don't know what your plans are, but I need you to get on the first flight you can find and come home" he instructed.

Kiara's heart skipped a beat. "Is everyone okay?"

"Yea, Dude, everything and everyone is okay," Kaanja responded casually. "Nothing to worry. Just come home as soon as possible."

With that he hung up the phone. Kiara knew better than to call him back. If he had decided not to share any more information than that, then there was no way she was going to get it out of him.

Kiara had been on the road for almost six months now, visiting different parts of the world to explore new opportunities to expand the business, as well as trying to decide on the ideal location for an overseas branch. Kiara had taken her Dad's business to another level through modernization and unique toy ideas. After extensive research on what clicked with the current generation of kids at different ages, she had come up with some ingenious toys that combined education with fun and were uniquely customized for cultural and economic sensitivities in different parts of the world. Her last three inventions had been highly successful globally.

She had a couple more countries to visit on her list, but for Kiara, family always took priority. She called her assistant to help rearrange her tickets and started packing.

❖

As soon as the door opened, Kiara was engulfed by all the nostalgic aromas coming from the kitchen. It was apparent that her Mom had been cooking up a storm, probably all of Kiara's favorite dishes. It had only been a few months, but it felt like years since she had been home last. She saw the tears of joy in her Mom's eyes as she hugged her.

The term home, sweet home, never rang truer. She saw the pride in her Dad's eyes as he engulfed her lovingly.

"Kaanja has an important meeting," he told her, "he couldn't get out of it. He wants you to meet him for lunch around two."

"Do you know why he asked me to come home?" Kiara's curiosity just could not be contained anymore.

"He asked you to come home?" her mom asked with surprise. "I was wondering why you cut your trip short. Thought you might have just gotten homesick."

"Well, whatever it is, I guess you'll find out before us as usual," her Dad commented happily. "Why don't you go freshen up and get some rest before you go. I'm looking forward to hearing all about your trip later!"

❖

Kaanja wasn't in the mood to give away anything yet. He sat across from Kiara on a four-person table with his unruly hair made unrulier by the wind, and his green eyes made greener by reflecting the Mediterranean Sea which spanned out in front of them.

"Something's been bothering you," he stated as if Kiara hadn't been away for the past few months. "Spill."

Kiara had long stopped being amazed by Kaanja's ability to read her. She only wished sometimes she could do the same when it came to Kaanja. He was a mystery she felt she was incapable of solving.

Kiara let out a big sigh. She needed to get it out.

"'Love is always there.' You know, you are the second person I heard that from, and it's been bugging the life out of me! I try to keep that in mind when I'm dealing with difficult situations and people, but it just doesn't ring true! Everyone doesn't deserve to be loved! And frankly, it's definitely not something you always feel naturally."

"How would you know?" Kaanja asked calmly. "We've come so far away from natural that we can't even imagine what natural is anymore."

"I don't get it," was all Kiara could say.

"We've been so indoctrinated from the day we're born about how we should feel about whom, what kind of love is appropriate or inappropriate, who to love and who not to love. The layers of ego we operate with has long smothered our natural instincts."

"How can that be true?" Kiara asked. "We've all experienced that when you meet some people you immediately like them, while with others you immediately dislike them."

"That has nothing to do with natural instinct. It's all about the brain being programmed non-stop," Kaanja responded. “We’re supposed to accept and love those we consider ‘family’ and be wary of all outsiders. Does that mean no family can ever hurt us, and that every outsider will? Of course not. Which is why our brain keeps building mechanisms to assess every individual in our lives against an expectation matrix, some of it imaginary. Is this person family? How much do I know her or him? Is the person from the same race as me? Same religion? Same country? What happened the last time I met a person like this? Etcetera, etcetera. There’s nothing natural about any of it. It’s all mental, even if most times in the subconscious.”

Kiara sat quietly and reflected on what she was hearing. She had experienced her first crush only because the guy had visually met her expectations about the person she would fall in love with. She had felt negative emotions towards her Dad’s relatives only because she knew how they had treated her parents. Okay, granted that what we feel is driven by the information in our brain, she thought, but isn’t that how it should be then? We can’t just love everyone indiscriminately. Especially those who don’t have our welfare in their minds.

“You want to love only those who make you feel good? That’s called selfish. If there’s one thing everyone agrees on about real Love, it’s that it is selfless.” Kaanja’s ability to read Kiara’s thoughts was plain uncanny.

"Let's do an experiment," continued Kaanja. "See that lady talking to the receptionist over there, probably about getting a table? What do you feel towards her?"

Kiara looked at the woman, simply but elegantly dressed, a pretty smile on her face, having a conversation with the receptionist.

"She's a pretty person, but I don't really feel anything towards her."

"Why? Because you don't know her? There it is. Your brain is programmed not to feel anything for anyone you don't know. Which is why when we meet someone where these programming barriers get overruled and we actually feel something for a person we don't know, we think it's special. But in fact, we're simply responding to that person based on a different set of criteria. Like say blond hair, if you're into blond hair."

Kaanja suddenly got up and started walking towards the receptionist while Kiara looked on with a sense of amusement. Kaanja was getting a bit too literal about his experiment. The lady who had been talking to the receptionist saw Kaanja and started walking towards him, her smile getting bigger and prettier. Kaanja gave her a hug and walked her to their table.

The surprise on Kiara's face was almost comic.

"Scarlett, meet my sister Kiara," Kaanja pulled out a chair for her as he introduced them. "Kiara, meet my fiancé Scarlett."

Kiara almost fell off her chair. It was not often that one saw mischief in Kaanja's eyes, but he seemed to be enjoying this moment immensely.

The next hour slipped by in a second. The paradox of time, Kiara found herself thinking, sometimes a moment seems to last a lifetime. Sometimes a lifetime flies-by in a moment. Kiara wanted to know every detail about the news, when they had met, how they had met, the road to proposal; every detail which Scarlett was only too happy to share.

When Scarlett left the table for a few minutes to go to the restroom, Kaanja turned to Kiara.

"So, how do you feel about her now?"

"I love her!" Kiara couldn't contain her excitement. She had considered a lot of possibilities about why Kaanja had called her back, but not in her wildest dreams had she expected this. She had always been sure that she was going to absolutely love whoever Kaanja chose to marry, because that was going to be a very special and important person in her own life.

"Well, I'm happy all it took was just one moment of deprogramming when I said the word fiancé. I rest my case. You see, Love is *always* there. It's just that you choose to experience it only when people meet a certain set of criteria in your head. If you rise above such physical level filtering, then you can experience it for anyone."

Kiara sat there quietly, reflecting on what she was hearing. No, it did not add up to her understanding of love.

"And while we're on the topic," Kaanja continued after a while, "let me also tell you about the so-called honeymoon phase. Right now you love Scarlett based on ten percent that you just found out about her, and ninety percent your mind filling in the blanks about how you desire her to be. Over time, as you find out more things about her, your feelings will shift depending on how much of the ninety percent matches up, or doesn't match up, to your expectations."

He let Kiara absorb that for another minute. He was breaking down her illusions, or rather delusions, about love. He knew that. But Kaanja wasn't one to beat around the bush. Every person must speak their truth clearly, that was his motto, and then let the other people decide whether it works for them or not.

"So," he leaned forward for impact as he made his last statement before Scarlett came back, "the real question to ask here is: if the type and degree of our feelings for others is directly proportional to the type of information being fed into our brains about them, real or imaginary, by us or by others, then is that feeling truly Love?"

Flavors of Love

STRANGER

When strangers donate blood
Or find some food for the hungry
When they help the blind to cross the street
Or give their lives for the country
For what, if not for Love?

6

In the Name of Love

Sounds of basketballs dribbling on the ground and bouncing off of the backboard filled the air. Five eleventh-grade girls stood in a line in the basketball court, taking their turn shooting the ball into the hoop and then jogging to the back of the line to do it again.

Not a single ball had been missed in the past five minutes, Kiara noted from the side bench. They were all doing so well. Kiara was volunteering as the youth mentor for these young girls who came from disadvantaged families. Their only hope for affording a good college was to get a sports scholarship. Kiara had been arranging a coach for them every weekend since her return back home almost six months ago.

The issue of educating girls was very near and dear to Kiara's heart. She was herself living proof of the positive difference education made in enabling women to stand their own ground with confidence and self-respect, and how it enabled them to contribute constructively in their own lives, in their family's lives, as well as to the economic well-being of their nation. The ripple effects of educating a girl were tremendous. It was unfortunate for the world that in so many parts the education of girls still remained a privilege rather than a birthright. Even if the economic affordability was there, the cultural barriers remained challenging. Kaanja had taken up this mission as his career focus, and Kiara made sure to give his organization her volunteer services to the extent possible.

She sat there on the bench watching the girls take their shot and admiring the courage they had shown in overcoming their circumstances. They had shown amazing wisdom in simply accepting the cards they had been dealt by Life at birth, and then picking up other cards with intention and determination so that they could play the game of life from a position of strength.

As practice time came to a close, everyone said goodbye to Kiara and left, except Cassandra. She came and sat next to Kiara, letting out a small sigh of dejection.

"What's up, Cassy? Are you feeling ok?"

"Yeah, I guess," Cassy replied listlessly. "I'm doing pretty good at this game, so I should be feeling good."

"But you're not," Kiara prompted, and when Cassy still didn't say anything, she continued.

"Have you ever noticed that it's always some thought in our mind that makes us feel the way we feel at any given point in time? Why don't you try to find the thought that is making you sad?"

They both sat quietly for what felt like a long time, only sounds of basketballs from other courts in the park countering the silence.

"I hate playing basketball," Cassy finally mumbled.

"Then why did you choose this particular sport? There were other options." Kiara asked.

"Given my height, my parents felt it would be the best thing for me to get into to help us get out of the dumps. My Dad started me on it since I was four seeing that I was the tallest kid in the neighborhood."

"Why didn't you tell him you don't like the game?"

"I didn't wanna kill his hopes. Life's not been easy. If I can help with a way out, then I have to do it. I know they want it more for me than themselves because they love me so much."

"Of course," Kiara's response was neutral, "of course they love you. They're your parents. Who can love us more than our parents? Which is exactly why it would be good to at least let them know how you feel about basketball, no? I'm sure they can help find a solution that's more in line with your interests."

"No," Cassy was firm. "My parents have invested too much in this for me to back out now. They want to see me become a professional basketball player. They'll be devastated if I quit. I can't do this to them. I love them a lot and I can't break their hopes like this."

"I don't doubt that you can go pro because you're really good," Kiara said honestly, "but how do you think your parents will feel when they find out that you sacrificed your own happiness to fulfill their dream?"

"Well, if I make it in this field and bring us out of our situation, then they'll feel proud and happy for me. When life's difficult, you can't really afford to follow your own dreams. You just have to do what seems practically right." With this, Cassy got up, said goodbye and left.

Kiara wondered if it would be appropriate for her to intervene with Cassy's family. She recalled her own pent-up resentments for not being taken seriously as the heir to her father's business because she was a girl, even though inventing new and innovative toys was her passion. She was lucky that she had Kaanja as her brother, who had intervened in the right way at the right time to make her Dad understand that he could not count on Kaanja to continue the business. He had convinced him that Kiara's ambition was more in line with the business, that she had the merit, and therefore there was no reason why she should not be the one to take it forward. He had made the whole family understand the value of pursing dreams, and how true happiness can be found in supporting each other in the fulfillment of those dreams while pursuing our own.

She took out her phone from her bag and called Kaanja. "Feel like shooting some hoops?" she asked without any preamble.

❖

Kaanja arrived fifteen minutes later carrying two bottles of water. He had moved out to his own apartment in anticipation of his wedding which was to take place in three months. He handed one bottle to Kiara and sat down next to her.

"This is not about shooting hoops, is it," he asked rhetorically.

"You have a girl named Cassy in one of your programs. I'm working with her to help her prepare for potential college admissions with sports scholarships. She plays basketball for her high school team and is highly talented according to the coach. But she hates the sport. She's doing it for her parents in the hopes of getting them out of their low-income status."

"Classic," was all that Kaanja said.

"She says they're putting the pressure on her because they love her and want a better future for her. She's doing it because she loves them and wants a better future for them."

"Isn't it amazing the things we do in the name of love," Kaanja again stated rhetorically. "We expect people to make sacrifices and be miserable so our self-interest can be served."

"But parents don't do it for selfish reasons!," objected Kiara. "They do it because they believe that's what's best for us."

"Yeah, Dude, they believe. On what basis, though? Do you think there has been any conversation between Cassy and her parents about what's best for her? What gives one person the right to decide what's best for another without even having a discussion about it? Parents generally opt for their own desire to be proud of their kid rather than the kid's happiness. They always forget how it felt when they were growing up and hoped their parents would just support them to discover their own unique talents and achieve their own ambitions."

"Are you now going to suggest that what our parents feel for us is not love either?" Kiara asked with a sense of dejection.

"No, because that's not true. Generally speaking, if there's anyone on this earth who loves us more than anyone else, it's our parents. They would die for us if they had to, but until they have to, the daily interactions in this physical reality is all about expectations. Sadly, more often than not, it takes a tragic situation for parents to realize how much they love their kids and how nothing else matters except their happiness. And by then, it's normally too late."

"So what are you saying?"

"What I'm saying is that every parent wants their kid to be successful; in many cultures, mainly boys. Globally, we haven't quite crossed the threshold as a society yet where women are expected to go much beyond managing a family. The definition of success is money, fame, power.

Happiness, satisfaction, contentment, sense of peace are grossly undermined. We forget that the end of it all for every single one of us is death, so when that moment comes, what is going to be the most meaningful accomplishment of our life? The money that we will leave behind? The fame that'll fade in a few days or months after we're gone? What will any of it mean if we don't feel a sense of peace and satisfaction about the life we lived? Such pity! There's this one miraculous opportunity we get to experience what we want to experience, and it gets blown away because everyone else thinks they know better."

"But it's true that there's a time that we're too young and inexperienced to know any better ourselves, isn't it?"

"Sure, which is why the whole creation system is based on having parents and/or guardians who can guide us and support us. They may not agree with what we desire, but every desire has a purpose in this universe. Not everyone is meant to be an Einstein. Imagine if no-one wanted to do truck-driving? How would we get our presents delivered? What if we didn't have janitors? Who would keep our school bathrooms clean? We must learn to treat every profession with equal respect. We need to let every desire thrive. That's all Life wants from us, to live fully and experience every unique combination of passion that is possible. The problem is that the profession an individual chooses is more often a product of pressure or last resort helplessness, rather than choice. Everything is driven by money, and the connection between money and a comfortable life has become too deeply ingrained in our economic system and in our minds to really be able to do anything meaningful about it at this point."

They sat there watching some kids shooting hoops in the next court, while partially lost in their own reflections. It was not often that Kiara witnessed Kaanja venting. The machinery of human existence had evolved in a very uneven and complicated way, and Kaanja was not immune to sometimes becoming frustrated when he was unable to break through it. One thing was clear to both of them, though: they weren't going to change the world by sitting here on the bench in a park.

"We're not going to the change the world," Kaanja offered, once again reading her thoughts. "We don't need to change the world. Everyone has the right to make the choices they want to make in life. You and I just need to do the best we can do based on our own beliefs and the circumstances we find ourselves in. And right now, we find ourselves in a circumstance where a kid needs some help to pursue her passion, without jeopardizing her chances for a more comfortable future. I'll talk to her parents and see if there is anything I can do to help. You, in the meantime, just focus on being my PIC for the wedding."

They parted with an affectionate hug. Kiara started walking back to her house with her mind already busy with all that needed to be done before the wedding. Kaanja had appointed her as his Person-in-Chief, which essentially meant *just tell me where and when I need to show up and in which outfit*.

Flavors of Love

MENTOR

Illustrated by Cynthia Medranda

That one encouraging word, when I thought I couldn't
That one inspiring push, when I thought I wouldn't
That one good kick in the rear, when I thought I shouldn't
Have all brought me here in life
Exactly where I want to be.

7

Love, Forgiveness, Justice

Terrifying sounds of loud crashes stunned Kiara as she was coming down the stairs, about to join her parents for dinner. The heart-rending noise of breaking glass followed, ending with a continuous blast of honking.

Kiara immediately dialed the emergency number before even checking what had happened. The sounds were indicative enough, and they were far too close for comfort. On the instruction of the person on the phone, she walked outside to assess the situation. It seemed a car had slammed into their neighbor's home. The driver was unconscious, his head lying on the steering wheel was causing the honking. A lot of screaming was coming from the house. Kiara's heart sank deeper as she suspected what might have happened inside.

The car had broken through the wall and the window on the front of the house, landing right into what was the Lorenzi's dining room. Their only son, Matteo, who was twenty-four years old, always sat on the window side seat for dinner. Kiara knew this because she had spent many evenings at their place throughout her life. Kiara was feverishly praying that no one would be seriously hurt as she walked towards the incident to see how she could help.

Before she could even ring the doorbell, the sirens of police cars and ambulances approached the house. She waited outside so that the medics could go in and get to work, then went inside and just hugged Mrs. Lorenzi. Her worst fear was playing out right in-front of her eyes. Matteo was lying on the floor, unresponsive to the CPR he was receiving, his mother screaming uncontrollably in Kiara's arms, his Dad talking to the medics to answer questions.

The driver of the car seemed also to be in critical condition. Everything was happening too fast to even absorb, and before long, both the driver and Matteo had been rushed to the hospital. Kiara's parents had joined her in the house, and Matteo's Dad had nervously requested them to please take care of Matteo's Mom while he went to the hospital in the ambulance.

Kiara held on to Matteo's Mom as they walked back to their own place so the authorities could start to seal the outside of the house for security. Dinner was forgotten on the table in both houses. Life had once more asserted its dominance by making everyone realize how unpredictable it is, and how no human, no matter how strong, how powerful, how rich, had any control over it. Everything had turned upside down in the blink of an eye for Matteo and his family.

Kiara was at a total loss as to what anyone could say to Matteo's Mom to calm her down. There was really nothing meaningful that could be said. Kiara's Mom just sat there holding Mrs. Lorenzi's hands and allowing her to cope in whichever way she chose; sometimes there would be loud sobs, sometimes indistinguishable words of prayer, sometimes just silence.

The house phone finally rang and everyone jumped involuntarily, almost afraid to answer. Kiara's Dad finally picked it up and when finished, informed them that the doctors had been able to revive Matteo but he remained unconscious. It was a ray of hope that everyone grabbed on to very tightly, each person in the room praying for him silently in their own individual way, sending Matteo positive energy as if trying to will him into consciousness.

❖

Kiara sat across the table from Matteo who was sitting in his wheelchair, a board of chess laid out between them. It had been six months since his accident; and it was going to be another six months of therapy before Matteo could even hope to walk on his severely injured right leg. He had been allowed to complete his MBA over the past couple of months through online participation, after which he had decided to focus fully on recovering before thinking about anything else for his future.

Kiara had made it a point to spend time with him over the weekends playing chess or cards or whatever else he was in the mood to do. He had been a good friend to her and Kaanja throughout his life even though he was a few years younger to them, and Kiara was determined to do everything she could possibly do to help him overcome this ordeal.

She was saddened but also amazed at the drastic change in Matteo's demeanor since his return from the hospital five months ago. He had lost the constant naughty spark in his eyes; his smile was no longer spontaneous; his words were wiser than his age. He had started reading a lot of books, books about the origin of life, the nature of the universe, and quantum physics. It seemed he had transformed from a young adult into a wise old man almost overnight.

"You know, I've been meaning to tell you," Kiara said casually as she moved her piece on the chessboard, "I'm so proud of how you're handling everything. I hope I'll be able to handle my life challenges with such maturity."

“Well, let’s hope you never have to,” Matteo countered her move by knocking off her bishop. “Such an incident in one’s family or social circle once in a lifetime is more than enough.”

Kiara thought silently about her next chess move, and then said, “I’ve also been meaning to ask you something, but it’s ok if you prefer not to discuss it.”

“It’s fine,” Matteo came back quickly, “I have no problem talking about anything. I’ve been thinking about things quite a lot myself.”

“Your Dad said you had no pulse for almost ten minutes. Do you have any recollection of that time period?”

Matteo stopped the play to sit back and recollect his thoughts. Time ticked away as he seemed to be lost in his internal reflections. “Funny you should ask that actually,” he finally spoke, “because it’s what I’ve been thinking the most about. It was so strange. It was like I had an awareness of just.....being, but I couldn’t see, feel, or hear anything....I was just aware of Being. It was the strangest thing I have ever experienced. It wasn’t an awareness of me as an individual, but me as the only thing there was..... just a piece of knowledge; no space, no time, no physics, no chemistry.....it’s hard to explain.”

Kiara didn't even pretend to understand because she couldn't. It reminded her of articles she had read from scientists trying to explain the moment before the Big Bang. Her own stance on the issue was that she didn't have time to understand these things at the moment; she had pushed them at the back of her mind somewhere as good pass-time activities once she was retired.

"I'm sure it's very difficult to explain such experiences in words if they somehow don't feel to be part of this physical reality," she acknowledged, then added, "but what amazes me most is that you don't feel angry."

"At whom? The person who did it?" Matteo asked, then continued, "I did feel angry while I was in the hospital. In fact, there were times when I felt so much rage that I felt I was falling over the edge into that same abyss again where everything disappeared and there was only the awareness of just being. Everything was just me; there was no one else there to blame."

A heavy silence fell between them, Kiara trying to process what she was hearing and Matteo wondering if she will suddenly start to think of him as weird. Kaanja would have been a better person to discuss his experience with, but he was now married and came only occasionally.

“Never mind all that,” Matteo sat up suddenly, “it’s your turn.”

“No, Matteo,” Kiara said gently. “I won’t pretend I get it all, but you have obviously been having some very strange but somehow significant experiences. I want to hear about them, and I promise I’ll try my best to understand.”

Matteo leaned back again. He needed to get it all out of his system and the only two people he felt he could talk to were Kaanja and Kiara.

Again a heavy silence fell while Matteo tried to organize his thoughts. Kiara got up and got them both a glass of water so Matteo wouldn’t feel rushed in any way.

“What I’m starting to realize is that everything that we feel, everything, it’s simply a mechanism for us to cope,” Matteo finally said softly. “Although we always associate the feeling with someone or something, it actually has nothing to do with them. People or things or situations may trigger us to feel a certain way, but ultimately it’s up to us and us alone to decide how we want to feel.”

Kiara remained quiet. It was best to just let Matteo get it out of his system.

"Take for example the issue of anger towards the person responsible for the accident. He was drunk. What he did was irresponsible. It was plain wrong. He must suffer the consequences of what he did. And he will. Justice has to prevail if we want to live in a society that is safe and runs in an orderly fashion and people don't think it's okay for them to behave in ways that can be harmful to others." Matteo stopped to take a sip of water.

"But my being angry, what's that going to solve? It'll have zero effect on the drunk driver who is in jail. He won't even know that's how I'm feeling. How he deals with his situation is his problem, but in the meantime, if I spend my energy on feelings that destroy my own sense of well-being, that would be just plain stupid. I'll end up constantly exerting all this negativity around me, which'll manifest into challenging situations in my own life, not in that driver's. I mean it's ok to get things out of your system by kicking, yelling, screaming if that helps to cope, but then you have to detach yourself from that emotion and move forward constructively so that all that negativity isn't regurgitated back to you someday." He stopped again to take another sip.

"I kept asking myself that if it's my choice to pick the emotion that helps me cope in the best possible way, then why would I choose anger? It creates so much stress. So I've decided to choose love instead; to choose forgiveness.

Not for someone else, but for myself. Love and forgiveness don't overrule justice. Justice is about the person who does wrong to someone else and must face the consequences of their actions. Love and forgiveness is about yourself, about you moving on with your own life, about you accepting the present and shaping your future instead of lamenting the past. The past is good for learning lessons, but if we keep reliving the past that is responsible for our present in our present moment, then Life will just continue to spill the same present into our future. How will the future ever change? We'll lose so much in terms of living the life we have, every moment, right here, right now."

Kiara sat there totally mesmerized. Such a complicated, loaded topic, yet how simply Matteo had explained it. She did actually understand it after all. She had heard similar words before: *Love is always there. Love is a choice.*

"Maybe it's true about the negative feelings," she asked after a while, "but when you love someone, it actually is about the other person, no?"

"No, not really. Different people will trigger different responses in you based on how your energies merge or clash. In some cases, the energies are so aligned that the only emotion that gets triggered is what we call love, which can be triggered not only by another person, but by anything in this Universe; watching the beauty of the sunset from a beach, a haunting melody, even a tragedy many times just shocks us into that state."

Kiara wasn't sure she agreed, so she remained quiet.

"When you experience Love," Matteo continued, "you will experience it as a healing energy for yourself. You start seeing the beauty in everything and in everyone else around you. If it's triggered by another person, it won't matter how that person feels or where that person is. You may not even trigger similar feelings in that person, but it won't matter. You'll be happy experiencing what you're experiencing. All your pent-up frustrations, resentments, anger, complaints, judgements slowly melt away. There are no expectations, no conditions, no demands. You see how everything is connected. You see the harmony in opposites. It changes you and your world in an amazing way because Love, the real one, is experiencing Itself through you, irrespective of the trigger. Love is what holds this whole creation together and enables everything else to be experienced."

Matteo closed his eyes, as if overcome by the emotion he was describing, then opened his eyes and continued, "Once we understand that others are simply a trigger for us, then we can exercise the freedom to enjoy what we're feeling if we want to, if not, we can ignore the trigger and choose to feel a different way. At the end of the day, all feelings are driven by our thoughts. Except Love. Love is always there to experience once we drop all the layers."

There it was again. Kiara hoped that someday she would actually be able to accept that statement fully, genuinely.

Matteo paused again for another second, then with a wistful smile, "I'm sure you're thinking that I've gone crazy."

A long silence fell between them again, each lost in their own thoughts.

Kiara finally sat up straight in her chair.

"Believe it or not, I actually understood every word you said. Seems I'm not as dense as I thought I was after all!" She laughed with feigned pride and then continued thoughtfully, "If anything, I think it's the rest of us who've gone crazy. We have created so many layers of complex equations around us that we've totally lost sight of the simple formula that governs Life: Love."

She then laughed again and added, "But you know what complicated people like us are good at? Beating simple people like you in chess! Your move."

Flavors of Love

SELF

Illustrated by Cynthia Medranda

Every dark thought, every thoughtless action
Every burning pain, every painful sorrow
Each a shining beacon, beckoning me to Me
Removing every layer, layers of all the pretenses
Pretenses of goodness, kindness, charity
That were suffocating the pure Love hidden beneath
Gasping to breathe.

8

The Love Trident

He pulled Kiara's hands with as much force as he could muster with his tiny body. "No, no, no! No sleep. Story, story, story!"

Kaanja's son, Ohru, was now five years old and always excited to see his Aunt Kiara, whom he had not seen recently in person for a while since she had been away for several months managing the overseas branches of her business. There was no way he was going to let this opportunity go by without hearing a story from his Kianty, as he called her. Although he was only five, Kiara had already sensed that Ohru was not interested in the children's fantasy and adventure books that abounded in his room.

He pulled her again forcing her to get up from her chair. "Story, story," he repeated, the words getting muffled with the air escaping from his shaky front tooth. Ohru loved his Kianty's stories because in her stories, Ohru always got to choose the character that he wanted to play, which made the story come alive for him in a way that no other did.

"Do you want the lights on or off?" Kiara asked once he was in bed and she was tucking him in.

"Off. If I want light I can just close my eyes," he said in his adorable lisp.

Kiara turned around half-way on her way to the light switch slightly amused. She didn't know what she had expected to see, but she felt a bit surprised by what she saw. Ohru was innocently just fluffing up his pillow so he could be more in a sit-up position for the story. He had simply stated what to him was a fact, without any idea about how that may sound like a paradox to adults.

"How will you see light if your eyes are closed?" she asked as she flipped the switch and came back to turn on the night-lamp next to the bed.

Ohru nodded his head vigorously as he said, "Ya, ya, I can see anything I want when I close my eyes!"

Kiara wondered if this was the time to explain to him the difference between reality and imagination, then decided against it and made a mental note to add this topic on her list of things to think about more deeply once she was retired. She had read several articles about quantum physics where it appeared the concept of reality was no longer as clear-cut as it once used to be. She needed to do more research before challenging Ohru.

"Today, we are going to live a story about three sisters, who were triplets," Kiara started as she pulled a chair to sit next to the bed. "You know what triplet means? It means three babies who were all born on the same day."

Ohru gave her a questioning look. "You mean their Mom brought home three girls from the hospital at the same time?"

Kiara smiled as she ruffled his hair. "Yes, but we'll leave that story for some other day. Today our story starts when they are already fifteen years old."

Ohru started counting on his fingers then took one leg out of the blanket and held up his two hands and one leg proudly for Kiara.

"Yes, that's right you smarty pants!" Kiara said as she tucked his foot back under the blanket. "Now what shall their names be?" Kiara asked.

"Oh, oh, I know," Ohru said excitedly. "Marta....Mindy.... and Mini."

"Okay, if that's what you want. You seem to like the letter M a lot," Kiara smiled.

"They're my friends in school. My teacher calls them the three musteers," giggled Ohru, unable to pronounce the word musketeers, and then started laughing hysterically trying to say the word again and again unsuccessfully.

Kiara saw him and started laughing uncontrollably as well. In her mind she was telling herself this is not even that funny, but she couldn't help herself. This was the emotion Ohru triggered in her and she just went with it because it was fun. They both laughed hysterically for what seemed like a long time.

Then Kiara took some deep breaths and continued.

"So the story is about the three girls and their Dad who wants to test them to see which one would be the best person to take over his coffee shop."

"Oh, oh, oh, can I be the Dad?" Ohru asked excitedly. "I will tell who to give the shop."

"Okay, sure. Then listen carefully because you'll need to think about everything you hear so you can make the right decision. Okay?"

When Ohru nodded vigorously, she started her story.

"One day, the father took all three girls to a safe, beautiful forest and gave them sleeping bags. He told them this was their adventure and they had to live there for one day and find food and water for themselves. Each one had to take care only of herself and not the others. Then he said he'll go for a walk, and left the girls alone. He found a place in the forest from where he could see what the girls were doing.

Marta left immediately in search of food. Mindy said to Mini that she would wait and see what Marta comes back with first. Mini said she was feeling lazy and she decided to take a nap."

Ohru was listening carefully. He knew he would have a decision to make at the end, and Kianty will ask why that one. She had explained to him the meaning of an informed decision some time back, and this was the part he loved the most about her stories.

"After walking for some time, Marta found an apple tree. She looked up at the sky and said a prayer of thanks for finding it. She was about to pick some apples from the tree but then she saw some good ones lying on the ground, so she just picked them up, leaving the ones on the tree for others. She ate many sweet and delicious apples until she was full. Then she took the seeds from the apples she had eaten, dug some holes in the ground, and planted them. Then she looked up at the sky again and said, 'Please make at least one of them grow into a tree so that when other people come to the forest in a few years, they would also be able to find food like I did.'

When Marta went back, she told Mindy about the tree. Mindy immediately got up and started running in the direction Marta had told her. When she found the tree she got really excited. So many apples! She ate a lot from the tree and then opened the bag she was carrying to fill it with as many apples as she could. Her Dad knew that she was planning to sell them and make some money. She also broke off many branches and stuffed them into her bag. 'I can burn these to stay warm in the evening,' she said smugly to herself out loud, 'I'm so smart!'

When Mindy got back, Mini had woken up. She was upset and asked Marta why she had to go get the apples herself when Marta had already brought some extra back. Marta told her she had to go get it for herself because that was what Dad had said, so Mini went. Mini didn't know which apples were ready to eat and which were not. She picked one up from the ground and took a bite, then threw it back because it was not sweet at all. She took one from the tree, which was also bitter. She started to get angry at her sisters. 'They took all the good ones and left the bad ones for me,' she complained loudly. 'They always get the best of everything.' Her Dad could sense her jealousy for her sisters. She got so mad that she took out her matchbox and set the tree on fire. 'If I can't have the apples then no one else can have them either,' she cried."

"Hmmmm," said Ohru while making himself more comfortable in the bed and closing his eyes.

"So, are you thinking about who to give the shop to?" Kiara asked after a few minutes. When no response came back, she realized that she would have to wait until tomorrow to get Ohru's decision because for the time being, he had already fallen into a deep sleep.

When she turned to leave the room after tucking him in properly, she was startled to see Kaanja standing at the door. She walked out quietly along with Kaanja, closing the door softly behind them.

"Where'd you hear that story?" Kaanja asked as they walked downstairs.

"I don't remember," Kiara responded, "Matteo's been giving me a lot of things to read and I started reading some of them during my flights. This story was in one of them. It stuck with me because I thought it was a simple enough yet educative one for children. I'll check with Ohru tomorrow to see how much of it he actually understood. If he didn't, then I can at least use it again to put him to sleep!"

"You know the story's about the three properties that govern this physical reality, right? The three faces of Love?"

Kiara looked at him with some confusion. "What do you mean govern? Like from beyond us?"

"Okay, Dude, that's a much longer story then! Maybe some other time."

Flavors of Love

CHILD

I know not where I come from, or where I need to go
I'm just glad you're here with me, helping me to grow
I see my smiles on your lips, I see my tears in your eyes
You're there when I take a fall, or let my spirits fly
I look at you I see no face, no gender, race, religion shows
I only see the selfless Love that beats, breathes, and flows.

9

Love In Disguise

Sounds of whimpering drifted outside Ohru's room as Kiara climbed the stairs. She had stayed over at Kaanja's so she could spend some more time with Ohru before leaving on her next trip. As she approached the room, she heard someone speaking in an angry tone, but the words were muffled.

She knocked on the door and opened it without waiting for a response. She saw Ohru's nanny get slightly startled by her entrance, but then she quickly got up from the chair she was sitting in and went over to start helping Ohru put on his socks. Kiara thought she saw Ohru wipe off tears as he ran away from the nanny to give his Kianty a hug.

"I was trying to teach him to get himself ready now that he's more than five," the nanny said with a flustered smile. Kiara felt the discomfort in the room as she picked Ohru up.

"Good morning," she said to Ohru with a kiss. "Are you ready for school? Your Mommy and Daddy went to work early, and they told me I could drop you off today."

Ohru screamed with pleasure. "Ya! I'm ready!"

Kiara collected Ohru's stuff, said goodbye to the nanny, put Ohru in her car, and started the fifteen minute drive to his school.

She couldn't shake off the dreadful feeling in her stomach as she looked at Ohru in her rear-view mirror. He sat there quietly looking out the window, his energy much subdued from what she remembered from a few months ago.

"So how do you like your school," she asked casually.

Ohru's face lit up as he said, "School is so fun! I've so many friends and we play all day!"

"Oh great! You had me worried. You were looking so sad I thought you didn't like school."

She saw his face drop again as he became quiet.

"Do Mommy or Daddy come to pick you up from school?" she asked.

"No, they only drop. Nanny picks me up at two. I have to stay with her until Mommy comes home at three." He got excited again, "Are you coming to pick me up today?"

"If you want," she replied. "So do you play with Nanny until Mommy comes home?"

Ohru said nothing and seemed to become lost in his own thoughts; his face looked as if he was going to burst in tears.

Kiara pulled the car over, turned off the ignition and went in the back seat to sit with him. She pulled him close to her.

"What's wrong, Sweety? You know you can tell your Kianty anything that's bothering you."

Ohru burst into tears and Kiara just held him until he quieted down. She wiped his face with her handkerchief and waited for him to speak.

"I don't like Nanny," he blurted out. "She's always yelling and she hit me." He burst into tears again.

Kiara was stunned, unable to believe how anyone could raise a hand at such a small, innocent child. As far as she knew, Ohru was a well-behaved kid; Kaanja and Scarlett had done a great job of instilling values and discipline. She felt a surge of rage towards the nanny run through her body.

"Did you tell Mommy or Daddy about this?" she asked when he had quieted again.

"No cuz Nanny said she'd tell them I was being bad and I wasn't even being bad. And then no other nanny'll come and then they'll have to leave me at home alone cuz they have to go to work."

Another burst of tears followed.

Kiara felt as if her heart was being wrenched out of her. How could this be happening with Kaanja's family. With Kaanja's son?! It wasn't fair. It just wasn't fair! If there was one person on this earth who did not deserve for something like this to happen, it was Kaanja!

She pulled herself together for Ohru's sake. What could this little kid have done at this little age to deserve this! She felt the surge of anger coming again, and took a few deep breaths to control herself.

"I'll pick you from school today, okay? You don't have to be with Nanny."

"Never?" Ohru asked expectantly.

"Never," Kiara replied. "But I want you to promise me one thing, okay?" She continued when Ohru nodded his head. "If ever someone is hurting you, I want you to immediately tell Mommy or Daddy, okay? They love you very much and they know you're a good kid. They know you'll always tell the truth, so you don't have to be afraid. They'll always be there to help you. And I'll always be there to help you, okay? If you're not able to tell Mommy or Daddy for any reason, come and tell me, okay?"

Ohru nodded his head vigorously and seemed to cheer up as his face started glowing with smiles. Then he asked again to make sure, "Kianty you'll come to get me later? And I can stay with you until Mommy's home?"

Kiara smiled and nodded, then belted him back in his seat before continuing the journey to the school.

❖

Kiara had never seen Kaanja truly upset, but as she sat across his desk in his office, she saw the blood rising to his cheeks as he gritted his teeth and clenched his right fist. She sat there quietly while he processed the information she had given him.

After a while he took a deep breath to calm himself and took out his phone to make a call.

"Can you please do me a favor," he said when the phone was answered at the other end, "Settle the nanny's account and tell her her services are no longer required. Thank you."

Kiara didn't know who he had called; probably his assistant since he would have had to explain a lot more to Scarlett.

"That's it?" Kiara asked when he hung up the phone. "You're not going to talk to this lady about what she did?"

"I will," Kaanja responded, "but it's not going to resolve anything at the moment. I need to do it when I'm ready to hear her side of the story as well without prejudice. All I know right now is that I don't want anyone looking after my son who's capable of hitting children, whatever the reason."

Kiara looked at him in disbelief for a second, but then reminded herself of who she was dealing with. This was not the time to press the issue, she thought, since she could see that Kaanja was trying hard to reset his emotional balance. It was the first time she was seeing him losing the battle.

He suddenly got up from his chair and made his way to the door. "I need to talk to Ohru. Let's go pick him up from school early."

❖

The issue of how such an experience could happen to people like Kaanja and Ohru continued to bother Kiara over the next few days. How could bad things happen to good people? she thought as she drove to her office. What was the point of being good and acting with love if you still got faced with such bad outcomes?

She wanted to make sure that Kaanja had taken some action against the nanny. She made a u-turn and decided to go to Kaanja's office instead.

"I still don't get how Life can be so unfair," she complained as she poured coffee for both of them. "Everything becomes so meaningless when bad things happen to good people."

"Well, you, my dear sister, came just in time to make the right intervention in my life, didn't you? What's unfair about that?" he asked.

"Oh, come on! That's just a coincidence," objected Kiara.

"Exactly! Coincidences are nothing more than the joint intersections we create with others based on the quality of the energies we exchange with them," Kaanja came back with conviction. "The Universe will use these intersections to bring the appropriate catalyst in your life, either to help or harm, depending on outcomes you've been generating for yourself throughout your lives."

"I don't buy that," was Kiara's response. "What kind of energy has poor Ohru put out there in this little time of his life that resulted in such an ugly outcome for him?!"

"First of all, the energies we put out there are eternally evolving and transforming, so it's not limited to a particular embodiment. But more importantly, remember the three governing properties I mentioned the other day? They're all present in this physical realm, and we all have to interact with all of them. It's nothing to do with being good or bad."

Kiara felt exasperated. "How can you downplay such a serious incident in your life? Your son's life, actually! I mean it's okay to get mad every now and then, and just let people have it sometimes when they deserve it!"

"And what will that solve?" Kaanja asked calmly. "You'll simply perpetuate the negativity. If there's a problem, it's better to exert your energy in trying to root it out from society. Otherwise, I may solve the issue for mine, but what about all the other children who might be suffering the same?"

Kiara gave up. "What three properties?" she asked with a sense of resignation. Deep down she knew that it was not Kaanja who needed to lower his wisdom, it was she who needed to raise hers. Yet at some level, she continued to feel the dissatisfaction of not being able to confront the nanny and give her a piece of her mind.

"Goodness or truth, attachment or passion, and laziness or darkness," Kaanja stated as he picked up his phone and told the person on the other end to move his next meeting by half an hour.

"Take a snake, for example," he continued after hanging up the phone. "Its nature is to bite and poison whatever it bites. It doesn't do it out of viciousness or spite. At the physical level, we all need to do things to survive; that's all the snake is doing. The thing is, we all live in the same physical realm. So if we come face-to-face with a snake, the snake's not going to think whether we're 'good' or 'bad' and therefore whether it should bite us or not. It's going to do what it knows how to do in order to survive. If we think we're so smart, then it's upon us to do whatever we can possibly do to recognize and avoid the snake. The problem is that there's no way we're always going to know at which intersection the snake might show up and why, but when it does, we just need to deal with it in the moment."

"You're saying that the nanny is the snake," Kiara provoked.

"I'm saying that we're all governed by these properties. Sometimes, we operate from a space of goodness, sometimes of darkness, and mostly of attachment in order to survive. We need to work with these properties in the best way we can, both in determining our actions, and in dealing with actions of others." Kaanja smiled, knowing Kiara was going to feel exasperated again. "You know what the beauty of it all is? These are just disguises of the original source energy to create experiences at the physical level." His smile broadened. "You know what the true property of the original source energy is?"

"Let me take a guess," Kiara said calmly. "Love."

"Exactly!" Kaanja said proudly. "Only when you operate from the space of Love, you are able to overcome all three physical properties. Not to say that you must overcome anything; experience all you want with all the properties in this physical realm. The point is that there's a choice you can make if you want to break out of the cycle."

He paused to let Kiara absorb, even though she was giving him her *'you're hopeless'* look. He didn't care. If there was going to be only one person that he might succeed in uplifting throughout his life, he thought, he would want it to be her.

"The nanny is obviously operating from a space of darkness, perhaps because she doesn't know any better, or because that's what she has chosen to experience, or she's helpless, or she doesn't think she has a choice. I do plan to speak with her because she needs to be made aware that her actions are unacceptable; it doesn't seem serious enough thankfully based on what Ohru told us for me to invoke the justice system, but someday it might become serious for her if she continues down this path. As they say, one's freedom to swing one's fist ends where someone else's nose begins. Either I'll be able to empower her in some way to make conscious choices in her life, or else she's free to create her own outcomes based on whatever energies she chooses to spread. Spreading darkness makes the world darker for everyone, including the person spreading it; it's this simple logic that sometimes seems to elude even the smartest among us."

Kaanja seemed lost in his own reflections, as if he was trying to internalize his own words. Then he continued.

“My takeaway is that from now on, every child I meet, I’m going to make sure I emphasize to them the importance of speaking to their parents about anything bothering them, no matter what anyone says to them. The problem I see, unfortunately, is that in the world we’re living in, sometimes the parents themselves are operating in a space of darkness and building abusive relationships.”

He seemed to be talking more to himself than Kiara. He paused again to gather his thoughts, trying to figure out the lesson he needed to draw from this experience.

“Children need to know that if they can’t talk to their parents because the parents are the problem, then they should approach anyone else around them and not be afraid to expose people. I know I, for one, am going to be extra vigilant from now on with every child I meet to see any signs of abuse or distress. Good news is that just as we have people around us operating from a dark space, we have even more people around us who are operating from a goodness space, so no one should be afraid to ask for help when needed.”

As Kaanja was speaking, Kiara herself was making resolves about how she would find a way to work on the issue of child abuse. So many children were suffering so much worse than what had happened with Ohru, but that’s a comparison only adults can make, she acknowledged to herself; to a child, any level of abuse can be traumatic.

"Children are so vulnerable," she said reflectively, unwillingly allowing the uplifting energy of the possibility of making a positive change because of the negative experience sweep over her. "They definitely need extra attention, but what about adults? So many adults are also trapped in abusive relationships."

"There's only one way out," Kaanja said with conviction. "Courage. Courage to stand up for yourself and the courage to stand up against another who is abusing you, no matter what the consequence, and no matter who the person."

"Easier said than done," commented Kiara.

"Yes, for sure. But there's no other way. At some point, you just have to choose to be courageous and face the consequences, which would most likely be less painful than the actual situation you're dealing with. No one should feel compelled to protect anyone from anything, least of all those who are operating from a space of darkness," Kaanja was firm.

"That's the irony of it, though, right?" Kiara commented, "that the victims think they're operating from a space of goodness by trying to protect others, like the family of the abuser."

"In reality, such thinking is a product of attachment," Kaanja clarified. "Goodness requires courage to stand up for what you judge to be 'right' and not allow or enable someone to expand their space of darkness because you're afraid of them."

"What if things become worse and more complicated for you as a consequence?" Kiara asked.

"That's where you just have to take a leap of faith. When your actions come from a place of goodness with a trust in the original source energy, then the outcome is infused with Love. The original source energy has nothing else to offer into the equation but Love."

He paused to see if Kiara was interested to hear anything more. It looked like she was, so he continued.

"No matter how you judge the consequence that unfolds once you've acted with courage, you need to keep the faith that it's all moving towards the 'right' place for you. Love resolves the situation in ways that we ourselves could not even have imagined as a possible solution. It may take time, but there's no other way for it to go when Love is in the mix. Courage is the only solution-oriented response to any kind of fear, be it fear of a person, fear of a situation, fear of failure, fear of an outcome, whatever; any fear can be overcome with courage, strengthened by a trust in the source energy of Love."

"If it's that simple, why is it so difficult," Kiara pressed, "and how do you teach someone courage?"

Kaanja's phone rang at that moment.

"That's exactly the question that you and I need to find an answer to." Kaanja got up from his chair and started to gather his papers. "Sorry, it's time for my meeting. We'll have to take this up another time. For now, thank you for being the torch-bearer in Ohru's life. I most definitely did some good things in life to land with you as the outcome," he said as he came around and gave her a big hug, "and for Ohru to land with his Kianty!"

Flavors of Love

PARENT

We thought miracles were a myth
And love so hard to find
We thought happiness was scarce
And life a complex twine
But then you came and taught us love
With simple happy smiles
In those innocent honest eyes
We see the miracle of our lives.

10

Entangled Love

Quantum Physics, that was the big heading on the wall as Kiara walked through the doors of the newest addition to their local science museum. Kaanja had asked Kiara to meet him there because that was his special gift to her on their thirty-sixth birthday. Although it felt like a strange gift, Kiara knew that when it came to Kaanja, it was probably not strange at all. In his view, the best gift one could give to anyone was the gift of knowledge so people could make aware choices in their lives. What better place to find reliable knowledge than in the field of science.

Thanks to Matteo, Kiara had been reading up a bit on the latest discoveries of quantum physics, which all seemed to point to the weirdness of this reality that we take so much for granted. On one side, she was happy to shrug them off as things that only happen in labs, but on the other, she contemplated at times that this whole universe is probably one huge lab where we living beings are serving as various experiments. Again, it was something for her to ponder upon after retirement.

Kaanja was already there at the other end of the huge room. When he saw Kiara walk in, he waved and signaled her to stay there while he made his way back.

"For you, we need to start from the beginning," he said as he gave her a hug and they both wished each other a happy birthday. "Prepare to be amazed!"

For the next couple of hours, they walked through the journey of the progress in quantum physics, beginning from the prediction of an atom by John Dalton in 1803. Kaanja took extra time to explain the discoveries he found especially interesting.

Although Kiara had been a bit skeptical about this visit at first, she couldn't help herself from becoming more and more intrigued as she saw the various exhibits. The concept of particle/anti-particle annihilation, the wave/particle duality of matter and light, the double-slit experiments proving that the act of observation changes the outcome, the deterministic versus probabilities debate on the nature of the universe, cosmic background radiation supporting the Big Bang theory, quantum tunneling where particles seem to pass through seemingly impassable barriers, heat crossing a vacuum by jumping from one fluctuation to the next across apparently empty space, the discovery of Higgs Boson which is dubbed as the God particle, and many other mind-boggling concepts.

When Kiara thought things couldn't get any more unreal and counter-intuitive at the quantum level, Kaanja turned to her and smiled with almost childlike excitement, "And now, the best for last!"

He walked her into a separate section that seemed to be a special add-on exhibit still in the process of being arranged, with the title Quantum Entanglement. Kiara read the introduction that Albert Einstein had described this phenomenon as "spooky action at a distance," in which two particles remain physically linked despite being separated across time and distances.

"For now, I want you to just understand what scientists have been able to prove," Kaanja said as they went from one display to another. "We'll do the non-scientific analysis over lunch."

❖

As they walked out of the museum, Kaanja said casually, "By the way, Matteo came back today from his trip. I told him to join us for lunch."

Kiara suddenly felt strange in her stomach as she tried to respond in a normal tone, "Oh, okay."

She hadn't seen Matteo for almost a year because he had a traveling job, and between his travels and hers, they had kept missing each other whenever either was back home. He did, however, send her occasional text messages just checking how she was, letting her know where he was, and sending some suggestions for things to read in her flights. Kiara, though she was not much of a reader, had actually started to buy some of the books; just out of curiosity, she always told herself.

When they arrived at the restaurant, Kiara was a bit relieved to see that Matteo was not there yet. Kaanja ordered their drinks and told the waiter that they were going to wait for another person before ordering food. He then turned to Kiara.

"So, what did you take away from the quantum entanglement evidence?"

"Well, I don't think it matters really what I took away. Why don't you just tell me what I should've taken away?" Kiara responded with a knowing smile. Her understanding was never going to live up to the depths of what Kaanja would have understood.

"Okay, if you insist," Kaanja leaned back in his lazy style. "In simple terms, when two objects have been in each other's vicinity, they get entangled for life. When you make any change to the first object, the same change takes place in the other object as well, no matter how far away it is and how much time has passed. There is instantaneous communication between them! We don't really know yet how that communication takes place, but we do know that it does, in fact, take place."

"Yes, it's quite amazing to have achieved that in theory or in a lab," replied Kiara, "but I have a feeling that you're about to make it very real for me."

"Just think about it," Kaanja was definitely excited, "It's already proven that this whole universe evolved from the Big Bang, right? We found the Higgs Boson that started it all; we know about the expansion of the universe from energy that just fluctuated from being nothing to being something, the Higgs Boson serving as the common seed, continuing to evolve until there's you, me, everyone else." Kaanja stopped to let the implication sink in.

Kiara found her brother's energy highly contagious. She sensed where he was going with this.

"You're saying that we're all ultimately entangled?" she said skeptically.

"Bravo!" Kaanja said proudly, leaning forward for impact. "Anything that causes an effect in one of us, affects everyone else in exactly the same way. It's just that we are operating at a much larger scale and therefore it's not so noticeable."

"Okay, so what's your point?"

"My point is that when people like me go around telling people that we're all ultimately one, they think we're crazy. But now science is proving that we're all connected in a much more real way. In my view, it proves why when a child is hurt, the mother feels the pain. In the case of mother and child, the entanglement is obviously very strong, therefore you feel the impact. The real truth, though, is that when one person is hurt, at some level everyone feels the pain, but because the entanglement is weaker it's not noticeable; or sometimes we actually do feel it but cannot understand why we're feeling sad, for example, or angry, or happy. Knowing that we're connected in a real, physical sense hopefully will help us to become more cognizant of how our thoughts, behaviors and actions affect others, and realize that at the end of the day, they actually affect us even more because they come around in a vicious or kind circle, whether we notice it or not."

"Yeah, I don't want to burst your bubble," Kiara replied with genuine regret, "but the thing with us humans is that we don't really care about things we don't notice...heck, we don't even care most times about things we do notice!" She looked at Kaanja and decided that she didn't want to burst his bubble. "I do get what you're saying, though. If we just stop and think about this for a second, there are deep implications about how understanding the way in which we are all connected can change the way we deal with each other."

"Remember our discussion the other day about the property of the original source energy?" Kaanja asked. "Love. It's what entangles us all. We don't notice it because we've covered it up with all types of egotistical, social, religious, mental, cultural, you name it, layers. If we strip these away, we'll begin to notice the Love entanglement which brought us all here."

"Okay, I guess that makes sense, although not so easy to do practically. Without those layers, we'll probably not be able to survive in this physical reality. In fact, we most likely donned those layers only so that this universe could evolve and we could survive in that evolving universe."

"Yes, I agree, completely. This is where the three governing properties come in. When Love fluctuated into Being, a mathematical formula with the three properties was put into motion that governs the evolution over time, continuously tipping the scale to find a balance, going from one extreme to another in the process."

Kiara reflected quietly for a while, at some level feeling the anticipation of Matteo showing up while trying to seem normal. "So you're suggesting that Love basically serves as the super consciousness driving everything with predefined mathematical formula. No free will."

"I didn't say no free will," Kaanja leaned back again. "The model will continuously adjust to ensure that the overall ratio of the three properties at any given point follow some predefined parameters. We can ourselves observe within our own lifetimes the shifting ratios that seem to have started with the goodness being the predominant one, to the present where attachment seems to be dominating most humans. Perhaps it's a cycle where finally the darkness property will become predominant and then it will start all over again by shifting to goodness."

"Okay, so where's the free will," Kiara insisted.

"At the individual level. At the individual level we might start our lives landing by chance at a point where, say, darkness dominates the other two, for example, but as an individual we can always redefine the proportions of the three properties within us by consciously adjusting our environment, friends circles, lifestyle, habits, thoughts, and most of all, mixing some Love into our actions."

"Yes, that," Kiara recalled. "You never answered my question though: if it's that simple, then why's it so difficult to do?"

"Because it's one thing to *know* something; quite another to have to *live* it. Our physical bodies are inherently lazy, therefore almost no effort is required to operate with the property of darkness, which is equivalent to laziness. It takes years of acting out of goodness to build up a reputation, but only a moment to have it all come crumbling down with one act from darkness. Darkness is the path of least effort. We can easily justify to ourselves why it's ok to just take or steal what we want, with no regard for anyone else. Such action, though, manifests as negativity and ignorance, and is driven by egotism, arrogance, and selfishness."

He stopped to check if he was making any sense to Kiara, then continued.

"Operating with attachment requires intellect. This property manifests as passion, action, drive, infusing a perpetual sense of always longing for more. It's also easy enough to work with because all you have to do is simply *react* to everything that comes your way, driven by self-satisfaction."

He paused again to allow time for reflection.

"Now, goodness. The goodness property is the closest to the original source energy and requires an awareness beyond the physical. It requires effort, determination, and most of all intention. It requires consciously acting rather than reacting. That's why it's the most difficult to live by as a default mechanism. If we put in the effort, though, it manifests as purity, knowledge and harmony, bringing joy, fearlessness, and contentment."

"Are you saying that the right answer is to always one hundred percent work with goodness?" Kiara asked.

"No, I'm not saying that. Even the universe doesn't function with one hundred percent of only one property. All three are crucial for the universe to grow and thrive, survive, and the changing ratios enable every possible experience that can be manifested, because ultimately, all this drama is only for Love to experience itself in every facet, without any judgment. The undeniable fact is that we cannot really appreciate light if we've never experienced darkness, or know what it is to be happy if we never knew what it is to be sad. At that source level, however, there's no good or bad, dead or alive, it's all just transformation of the original energy field through interactions with the physical properties."

"So no free will, really," Kiara pressed again.

"There's total free will for us, in this reality, to find the desired balance at the individual level; the freedom to do so is built within the model. Don't worry about the universal level proportions that need to be maintained by the model, the universe will take care of that without violating your freedom to choose at the individual level. Our choice of the properties shapes our thoughts, which in turn shapes our actions, which in turn shapes our lives. These properties are therefore our tools to create the experiences we desire."

He paused again to let it all sink in, while Kiara wondered where this was all leading to.

"If we don't influence the balance consciously ourselves, then we'll simply go along with the universe's proportions with a feeling that we have no control," he continued. "The three properties will eternally entangle with each other to take turns having their day in the sun because based on the model, every single combination and permutation must be experienced; an eternally unsolvable equation because you can continue to add another decimal point to any number you're working with, forever."

Kiara started to get a distinct feeling that this was all definitely leading to something important.

"If we just react instead of acting consciously," Kaanja continued, "we will blame or credit the universe for all outcomes, be it what we call *good* outcomes or *bad* outcomes. Creating the experiences we desire at the individual level becomes much easier when we go deep within and reconnect with Love, which can then enable us to instantaneously reposition ourselves on the universal map, and recalibrate our use of properties."

"This is all a very interesting theory you have," Kiara relented grudgingly, "and I'll certainly try to test it out, because until I do, I've no business arguing with you about whether it works or doesn't. But you actually have a reason for telling me all this, don't you?"

"I just always want you to remember that Love *is* always there. I want you to always consciously make sure you overrule the universe's proportions with your own when the preset ratio is not working for you. In all your relationships, press the reset button whenever necessary so that the layers don't keep accumulating over Love."

Kaanja suddenly sat up straight again and seemed to study her more intensely. "But you're right, that's not why we're here," he said purposefully. "Think about those entangled photons. We can experience the entanglement somewhat strongly when there's a direct connection, like our blood relatives. We experience love at different levels depending on the mix of the three properties within us and within them. When our energy fields merge during any interaction, we experience it beautifully when no layers are covering Love, or not-so-beautifully when the predominant property is either attachment or darkness. In general, we humans are typically quite lazy when it comes to working on relationships. We never want to remove the layers that'll allow Love to come through, because the ego grips us mercilessly."

Kiara almost felt the intensity of his words run through her body.

"But imagine when some particles that were direct partners, meaning split from one particle and separated during the expansion process, suddenly by chance find themselves manifested in different bodies on earth? Although by chance, imagine the experience it creates for Love! This is actually when we see those rare but beautiful relationships, be it between a mother and child, between siblings, friends, relatives, partners. It doesn't really matter the relationship. This is when the purity of Love shines through in all its splendor, and a beautiful experience is able to manifest in that relationship."

"Well, you and I definitely share that split photon," Kiara laughed, "because sometimes you seem to just read my thoughts before I've even formulated them myself!"

Kaanja smiled. "Other than me, is there another photon in your body that's perhaps split and entangled somewhere else in a different type of relationship?"

Kiara was taken by surprise and suddenly felt the nervous tension in her stomach again. "What do you mean?" She tried to sound casual.

Kaanja leaned forward and took her hands in his. "You know, Sis, there might be a mathematical formula that this universe is eternally solving, but Love has no rules, no predefined parameters, no properties. It doesn't care about age, religion, gender, nationality. It just Is, and rejoices in itself through any entity where it's able to shine through with purity. That level of connection is very, very rare in our reality, and is therefore quite easily visible when it shows up."

Kaanja had never addressed her as Sis; it had always been Dude. This was serious, thought Kiara. She didn't know how to respond. She hadn't really thought about it much herself, but realized at that moment why she had been avoiding it....she was about five years older. She stopped herself with a sense of shock: wait, why was she thinking about that? Kaanja hadn't even brought it up!

Kaanja kept her hands in his, and said, "When he shows up, I want you to sort it all out with him, okay?"

Kiara felt the blood rising to her cheeks. She wanted to pretend she had no clue what he was talking about, she wanted to deny what he was suggesting, she wanted to seem normal or be upset with him for bringing it up. Eventually, she just gave up and simply looked at him and nodded slowly.

"How were you so sure about me?" she asked, just as the restaurant door opened and Matteo walked in with a bouquet of flowers in his hands.

Kaanja downed the last gulp of his drink and wiped his mouth with the napkin. "I wasn't," he said with an impish grin as he got up to shake hands with Matteo.

Flavors of Love

FAMILY

The sun burns, the earth churns
The wind blows, the water flows
Some cow's milk, some weaver's silk
Some farmer's crop, some stranger's shop
I see the links so clearly
Why we are all One family.

11

All is Love, Love is All

Kiara felt her heart skip many beats as she got up and gave Matteo a hug. He handed her the bouquet and smiled broadly.

"Happy birthday," he said, then turned to Kaanja, "Happy birthday, but no flowers for you."

Kaanja pretended to be offended, then picked up his phone and sunglasses from the table and looked at Kiara with his deep, penetrating eyes. "Unfortunately, I have to go for an important meeting. In any case, whenever I see Matteo, he only talks about you, so you guys may as well just talk to each other." He turned to Matteo, "The reservation is for two and it's already on my account, so no need to worry about all that. Eat your heart out."

He shook hands with Matteo again and then winked at Kiara and said, "Happy Birthday." With that, he turned around and walked out as if it was all such a normal thing to do. It began to slowly dawn on Kiara that this was all a set-up.

Matteo sat down and they both sat silently for what felt like an eternity. Surprisingly, it did not feel awkward at all. Matteo finally spoke.

"You know what, I think I can beat you in chess now. I've been practicing with a very smart computer."

Kiara laughed. "No chance, but you're welcome to try!" She couldn't help but notice his strong jawline as he ordered food for them. She thought about her initial yardsticks for the *right* person for her. Matteo was probably too tall in comparison. Dark? Not at all. Handsome? Well, not really, but definitely attractive. Nevertheless, the feeling of being connected had always been there. For Kiara, the realization of his significance in her life was not a sudden discovery in the present moment; it was more like an acceptance of what had always been there but constantly been pushed behind different layers of logic.

Once finished with the waitress, he turned to her, "There're a couple of dishes here that you must try!"

Kiara didn't know where the time flew as they ate and talked. There was so much to catch up on; work, travels, books, the weird quantum discoveries.

It was only when Matteo's phone rang that they realized that the restaurant was almost empty. He excused himself to take the call, and walked outside while gesturing an apology to Kiara.

Kiara just sat there and savored the moment. Nothing had changed, really, and yet nothing was the same. She thought about how every moment she had to wait for that weekend time with Matteo during his recovery had always felt like a lifetime, and how it now felt like she had lived a whole lifetime in every moment of the past couple of hours. She had never in her life felt as if she was lost, and yet right now it felt like she had suddenly found herself. Nothing new had been added into her life from the external world, yet everything seemed new as soon as she allowed the feelings that had always been hiding deep inside her to surface freely.

She didn't even realize when Matteo came back as she sat there with a faint smile on her lips, lost deep in reflections. She was startled by Matteo clearing his throat.

"Sorry to interrupt your thoughts," he said as he sat back down. "I didn't even realize how late it is and I was supposed to be at a very important meeting fifteen minutes ago."

"Oh, we should get going then," Kiara said as she started to get up, but he stopped her.

"In a few minutes," he said as he looked deep into her eyes and said, "We have a lot more to talk about, but this is not the right place."

Kiara just looked down at her hands as the blood rushed to her cheeks again. She didn't know what to say, so she said nothing. A comfortable silence followed as Kiara looked up again. Wow, she thought, how was it possible for two people to say so much to each other without even saying a single word? Must be the entangled photon, she joked to herself silently and almost laughed out loud.

Matteo finally spoke. "Dinner tomorrow? You can tell me the joke then."

Kiara smiled and nodded. Matteo got up to pull out her chair as she got up and then handed her the keys to his car. "Here, you drive home. I'll catch a cab."

In total silence he walked her to his car, closed the door after her, waved goodbye and walked away to hail a cab.

❖

Kiara turned the car into the parking lot of the botanical garden and turned off the ignition. She just sat there for a while wondering why she had come here. She was really not the botanical garden type, but she needed to be alone for a while. She got out and bought the ticket. A nice walk in a nice place was what she needed, she told herself.

Stop and smell the roses. How many times had she heard that phrase from Kaanja. Today, she actually did it. She noticed the beauty of the petals that hugged each other to create the overall mesmerizing effect, yet every petal beautiful in its own right. She could have sworn that it was trying to communicate with her as the fragrance soothed her mind.

She sat down on the grass under the cherry blossom tree and looked up at the beautiful pinkish-white umbrella that shaded her from the sun. It felt as if it had been put there just for her, just for this moment; another long separated photon that had been waiting for years in this garden for her to show up.

Her mind started drifting to the relationships in her life. She thought about her Dad. Although all was well now, she had been unable to completely purge the deep-down resentment she felt towards him for the initial restrictions she had faced in her life only because she was a girl. It was embedded somewhere inside her in a way that she had just accepted that it will forever remain a part of who she is; she had left it there and moved on. At this moment though, she saw clearly the love that had driven him to be that way. He had allowed his love to manifest as fear in his daily thoughts and actions, letting attachment dominate. An incredible wave of energy swept through her whole body; she felt the tears surging up in her eyes as if to cleanse her whole system of any negativity towards her father.

She thought about her Mom. If there was any natural occurrence on this Earth of Love being covered by the least amount of worldly layers, it had to be within a mother; so unselfish, unconditional, not always totally devoid of attachment and expectations, but Love always nudging these properties in favor of the child's well-being and happiness. Kiara felt an immense sense of gratitude for being so lucky to have a Mom like the one she had. She wished her Mom was there with her right now, she would have given her a really tight hug and said thank you.

And what to say about Kaanja. If there was ever a direct split of a photon separated in two literally entangled human bodies, it was her and Kaanja. She never had to tell him anything; he just always knew. She benefited from the fact that he was wise enough to always choose goodness to guide his actions. She herself had been leaning more towards attachment, and perhaps often times even darkness, but lately she had been understanding that

Kaanja's positive choices were helping her much more than her negative choices were harming him. His energy field had enough positive force to keep the state of both their lives in a happy balance, giving Kiara enough space to experiment with the darker properties of the universe without any serious impact on Kaanja, or even on herself. She tried to feel angry at him for what he had done today without first checking with her, and on top of it, tricking her into admitting what she had not even admitted to herself yet. But she couldn't. His state of Being and positive force in her were far too powerful for her to cut through and superimpose it with her own. Love had always been able to shine through unhindered between them; he was the best brother anyone could ask for. Nevertheless, she *will* find a way to get back at him, she decided with an affectionate smile.

She got up and started walking towards the huge fountain, enjoying the cool spray that rushed to welcome her. She looked up at the sun bombarding all those photons down with all its strength, and yet she felt the rays penetrating her skin like a soothing balm. She stopped walking, unaware that she was actually getting wet. She recalled what she had learnt at the museum and was almost dumbstruck by its very real implication. Every day of our lives the rays from the sun are absorbed in our bodies, directly contributing to our good health, not to mention our survival. The sun is not just entangled with humans, but with every single element of this Earth, and directly enabling the planet's sustenance. For what does the sun burn, she thought, if not for Love? And what other physical manifestation do we need of the all-permeating Life force before we will choose to believe in that supreme energy that drives the Universe?

She started walking again, using her hands to wipe the water off her face, then stopped again as she looked at her wet hands. It was almost as if she could *see* the water seeping through into her skin. Oneness with nature had never felt so natural. Everyone and everything in this universe is so connected and held together by that one source originating energy, she thought, so codependent on each other for survival. We see such clear examples of it all around us every day, she thought, and yet how do we never even notice or acknowledge them? She found her total awareness engulfed in a surreal feeling of gratitude, gratitude for every element in nature that was enabling her to have this experience. She realized that if there was one worldly layer through which Love actually filtered through unhindered, it was gratitude; a sense of gratitude was as effective in melting layers as Love itself.

She didn't know when she had started walking again, but suddenly she found herself inside the rainforest simulation area. She had run out of things to reflect on; it was time to face the one that she had been subconsciously avoiding.

She allowed her mind to drift to Matteo, and felt a wave of energy flow through her that she could only define as healing, soothing, coming home. She felt a sense of wholesomeness within herself, but not the way in which she had heard people talk about how the other person made them feel complete. She felt complete within herself. She looked down and stared at the grass beneath her feet. For a second she thought she could almost *see* again that every blade was complete with the full power of the source energy. What if, come tomorrow, Matteo told her that Kaanja had totally misunderstood him, she wondered. It wouldn't make a difference, she told herself with complete honesty. She knew that the amazing transformation she was experiencing within herself was always going to remain with her. It was not dependent on anyone else.

Matteo was the trigger that had lifted her to the next level of awareness. He had played his very critical role in her life. The rest will be whatever it turns out to be, she thought, as Matteo's words from several years ago came back to her with crystal clarity.

If it's triggered by another person, he had said, *it won't matter how that person feels or where that person is; you may not even trigger similar feelings in that person, but it won't matter. You'll be happy experiencing what you're experiencing. All your pent-up frustrations, resentments, anger, complaints, judgements will slowly melt away. There'll be no expectations, no conditions, no demands. You'll see how everything is connected. You'll see the harmony in opposites. It'll change you and your world in an amazing way because Love would be experiencing itself through you, irrespective of the trigger.*

Her mind drifted back to her first experience with what she had thought was love. She felt no regret nor any negativity towards the person. It was clear to her that her current experience would not feel so fulfilling if she hadn't had any prior experience of what love is not. If only we could know this difference without having to go through some heartbreaks, she mused.

Kiara sat down on a bench with sounds of rainfall all around her, even though she couldn't see or feel the rain. There were no words to explain the feeling she was experiencing, the closest she could find was 'bliss.' It needed no words or explanation; it was something that could only be experienced. She understood deeply how it could only be experienced within a physical embodiment, though. Without the physical embodiment, Love was merely a piece of abstraction.

She reflected that one does not have to be in love to cut through the layers and see this Truth, but being in love definitely fast-tracks the process. Given Love's nature to communicate without any time-lag, when given even a small opening, which typically happens when people are in love, it melts away all the layers instantaneously. She finally understood intuitively how thoughts and actions driven by the three properties always try to take control and layer it up again and try to push Love in the background to create diverse experiences, and she could also finally *see* that Love is indeed always there. Always. Just waiting for someone to use their freedom to choose it. The instant this choice is made, Love fluctuates from being a piece of abstraction to Being, manifesting in the physical realm. Everything else then just falls into place to create fulfilling experiences.

Kiara looked around, breathing-in the beauty around her, tears starting to roll down her cheeks uncontrollably for no apparent reason, a radiant smile refusing to leave her lips.

There was nothing but Love all around her. Love vibrant with Life everywhere. Experiencing Itself in every possible manifestation, yet remaining pure, unattached, untouched, always waiting to be called upon to fluctuate into yet another experience.

Flavors of Love

ROMANCE

Illustrated by Cynthia Medranda

The heart skips a beat,
Then beats at twice the speed.
The knees go weak and buckle,
The smiles become so subtle.
The stomach flutters like butterflies,
The brain no longer wise.

12

When Love is Not Enough

"Love is always there, Love is always there, Love is always there," chanted Kiara under her breath as her cheeks flushed with anger and her hands balled into a tight fist. She had adopted these four words as her mantra for whenever she felt like she was losing control of her emotions. She took a couple of deep breaths and closed her eyes tight while she sat crossed-legged on the sofa, then her lips continued: Love is always there, Love is always there!

"Oh screw it!", she gave up and got on her feet to confront Matteo. "Life is not some fairy tale with a happy ending all the time just because someone's a good person!" she blurted, trying to control her volume. "You have to be practical. You have to be smart. You can't just let everyone take advantage of you! Sometimes Love is *not* the right answer."

Kiara and Matteo had been married three years now. If anything, their love had only grown stronger, but that didn't mean that some of Matteo's habits did not often create layers for Kiara; it was becoming more and more difficult for her to immediately allow Love to melt them. Life demanded a lot more than Love sometimes.

Matteo gently sat her back down. "No one is taking advantage of me," he said as he sat down next to her. "She needs help. I *want* to help."

Matteo was too good for his own good, thought Kiara. He didn't even realize it when people were taking advantage of him. She could see it so clearly. Everyone in his life thought they could call upon him whenever, wherever, and for whatever. As if he had no life of his own!

"It's not about right or wrong answer," Matteo added. "It just takes more than love to solve a situation in this world. Love without action is useless. We can't just sit here feeling love and talking love and do nothing. If we don't act, it's all meaningless."

"We promised Ohru we'd be there for his moving up ceremony," Kiara tried to be reasonable, "That's much more important for me. Kaanja should be here any minute to pick us up!"

"Yes, and you should go. I'll make it up to Ohru, I promise. Right now, I *have* to do this. Please understand."

Kiara was in no mood to understand. The darkness property was winning the battle, and Kiara didn't want to fight it. It was just too exhausting to constantly be aware of how you're behaving and consciously override it. It felt much better to just be mad and vent, to just live the moment in all its ugliness.

Before she could say another word, the door bell rang. Kiara picked up her stuff, opened the door, walked out, and slammed the door behind her.

Kaanja walked behind her to the car without saying anything. Kiara was relieved to see that there was no one else in the car since she was in no mood for chit chat, and she didn't want anyone to see her in this state.

"Dad took everyone else to the school because Ohru needed to get there early," Kaanja said once they were on the road. When Kiara said nothing, he continued, "The last thing we should do is to replay whatever it is in our mind over and over again and keep feeding the emotion until it completely takes control of our thoughts and actions. Especially if it's on the dark side." He paused for a moment, and then raised his volume a little, "Dude! Welcome to the present."

“There’s no need to shout,” Kiara finally responded, “I can hear you.”

“Well, you could’ve fooled me! Wanna talk about it?”

“No.”

“Okay then, don’t talk about it to yourself either. It’s a waste of energy. No one’s listening. Although sometimes, as you know, I can hear it.”

Kiara sighed. “So what are you hearing now?”

“My crystal ball tells me you and Matteo had a fight,” Kaanja revealed with a fake flare, feigning suspense.

Kiara just stared at him, totally unamused.

“Okay, okay, drop the look, I’m not ready to die yet!”

Kaanja put on some nice soothing music as they drove in silence. Kiara took a deep breath and allowed the music to sweep through her. *Feelings and emotions are nothing more than an expression of one’s thoughts*, someone had once said to her. *What needs to be controlled are the thoughts, not the emotions.* As her thoughts focussed on the music, her emotions started to transform automatically.

"I really, really wanted Matteo to join us today," Kiara volunteered calmly as they stood at a red light. "He had other priorities. Last minute, and people I don't even know."

"Okay," was all she got from Kaanja.

"He's always giving priority to other people," Kiara continued. "Like what about us? We're family!"

"Without passing any judgement either way," Kaanja offered in a neutral tone, "because I've no idea what that other priority is, can I just say that priorities have more to do with the gravity of a situation rather than with family or non-family? It's also true that we often count more on our family to be the ones to be more understanding."

"You mean family should not always be one's priority?"

"Always? No. Life can't work that way. Let's take a stark example, although we both know things are not always so starkly black or white. If you have only one small bottle of water and your kid is standing there with muddy hands to be washed, and a poor thirsty stranger kid is standing right there asking for water, what would you do?"

"That's different," Kiara complained.

"No, it's not. It's always a matter of choosing which situation we want to resolve, driven very much by the physical property that is dominant within us at that moment. Even in the situation I describe, the response is not obvious. Many people will choose to ignore the poor kid and find a valid justification for it. It's always a matter of individual choice. You have the freedom to choose your response, but you can't expect that others should also choose to respond in the same manner, family or not."

"Then what's the point of marriage if we continue to make individual choices anyways?" Kiara asked with some annoyance.

"Marriage definitely doesn't mean that you both become the same person," Kaanja said patiently. "Each will still have their own likes and dislikes, perspectives, judgements. That doesn't mean they need to constantly clash with each other. Marriage provides the space for co-existence of different experiences if we allow Love to guide the path. You remember Love? The thing that's always there?"

"Okay, Mr. Know-it-All," Kiara said as she started to feel that perhaps she could have handled the situation differently. "So what's the right answer?"

"What's the question?" asked Kaanja.

"Co-existence of different experiences. How?"

"Oh, that's pretty simple. The things you enjoy doing together, you do them together. The things you enjoy doing separately, you do them separately. Marriage definitely doesn't mean that you have to do *everything* together. You need to give each other the space to enjoy things separately with others in your lives, or prioritize things based on your own sense of judgement. Sometimes this'll mean that you get to be second, and that's fine. There will be many times when you'll be first. These life choices should not be confused with Love. When Love is chosen to flow in a marriage, such understanding of each other's space becomes easier. One of the things that destroys a marriage is precisely the expectation that there can be no separate fun time or prioritization."

Kiara said nothing, quietly absorbing what Kaanja was saying. Of course Matteo wouldn't have enjoyed the ceremony while thinking all the time of the person who needed his help. He had made the right choice. She probably would have made the same choice, or would have regretted it later if she hadn't.

The flow of Love as the underlying connection in her marriage was abundant, there was absolutely no doubt in her mind about that. She just needed to manage her thoughts better in the future to not burden this connection with selfish expectations. The Love that she and Matteo had uncovered was clearly not something that could be limited between two people only. They had discovered the Love which permeates through everything that exists, manifests everything that exists, encompasses even that which doesn't yet exist. This Love will always drive them to resolve a lot of situations for a lot of other people, she thought. It will inspire them to make choices that will go beyond each other in order to empower Life itself. She knew Matteo will always be standing next to her in all her decisions that uplifted Life for anyone, because they both understood the circle of connection which motivated them to act.

Kiara picked up her phone to call Matteo as she resolved to make sure that their Love never gets overshadowed by thoughts arising from attachment or darkness. She was going to do everything possible to make sure that Love always shines through all their ups and downs in life.

She closed her eyes, took a deep breath, savored the feeling of just Being, and said to herself: *I choose Love.*

Flavors of Love

GOD

Webb's First Deep Field, galaxy cluster SMACS 0723
From where we all came - Face of Love - 4.6 billion years ago

When Light desires to express itself, Darkness comes to being
For without darkness, light has no purpose.
Desire grows for more expression, each experience another layer
Pushing Light beneath the surface.
When Desire can no longer see, and craves for Light to shine through
Suddenly, everything falls back into place.

Epilogue

Nothing to see, yet so much remains unseen.

Nothing to hear, yet so many sounds just waiting to find an ear.

Nothing to smell, yet a plethora of odors trapped in a vacuum.

Nothing to taste, yet the immense possibilities of flavors lying dormant.

Nothing to feel, yet imagination running rampant with thoughts of what could be.

Nothing.

Nothing but an awareness; an awareness of being.

Just Being.

But being who?

Suddenly a big explosion. Sights, sounds, odors, flavors, emotions propelled into an expanding space, colliding, attaching, merging, splitting; traveling billions of light years, over billions of eons, finally sprouting into Life.

And then finding a home.

A girl closes her eyes to see the light of Truth, takes a deep breath to find her emotional balance, savors the moment of reconnecting with her source, feels the calmness of her true Self, and smiles happily as the words vibrate through her being: *I choose Love.*

Just Being suddenly awakens, fluctuating into action, shining forth brightly through her – finally able to see Itself through her, able to hear Itself through her, able to get a whiff of Itself through her, able to know Its own flavor through her, able to love Itself through her.

Able to *live* what it *knows* Itself to be.

Love.

****

ABOUT THE AUTHOR

I am You. You are Me. My whole life has been a learning of how we are all connected - have been from the time of our existence, from the time the Universe came into Being. Any other introduction in terms of nationality, education, profession are meaningless.

Separation is an illusion we must rise above to live a meaningful life at the physical level. The first step is to discover our true Self.

When you find yourself, you will realize that everything else is already here: Peace, Love, Happiness. I hope to spread this understanding with my books. Finding fulfillment is much easier than it might seem at first.

Love is calling; all you have to do is answer the call.

You may also want to answer the call of Life with my previous book: Life Calling.

All proceeds from both the books, and any further books I may write, will be used to send disadvantaged girls to school. Education and equal opportunities are key to making our world a better place for all of us. If you know a little girl who should be in school, recommend her at EducateEveryGirl.com.